Introduction

This guide exists to help make [illegible] excellent 'all ability' trails that exist for those le[illegible] to visit some of the most beautiful places in North Wales. S[illegible] the trails described [illegible] get to places high in the mountains as, for example, to Llyn Llydaw below the dramatic pyramidal peak of Snowdon, with the 1,000 feet high cliffs of Lliwedd to the left and the castellated Crib Goch ridge high up to the right. One trail visits some of the tallest trees found in Wales, a couple have added nature puzzle trails whilst others just explore the beautiful countryside with some really stunning views. By their nature the trails are easily and clearly followed ,needing little navigational knowledge.

All ability trails are generally wide, usually have a good surface and are reasonably level for manual wheelchairs. Only the power of arms or helpers will be the limiting factor as to how far one travels. The Mawddach Trail is a good example of this. I have split the description of this into five different sections each requiring a return to the starting point. These are 1, Dolgellau to Pont y Wernddu; 2, Pont y Wernddu to Penmaenpool; 3 – Penmaenpool to Gwynant; 4, Gwynant to Arthog and 5, Morfa Mawddach to Barmouth. However, the entire trail can be completed from Dolgellau to Barmouth, or vice versa, in a single push, a distance of 10 miles. This would require a pick up at the far end, or the trail can be undertaken as a round trip of some 20 miles! I have not described the section from Arthog to Morfa Mawddach in this guide because this is, in my opinion, by far the least interesting section.

On off-road terrain the capabilities of different models of wheelchairs have a much greater influence on what is possible. The level of assistance that the user feels is acceptable also influences what the user considers as do-able. *Scooters* can access steeper off-road trails whilst *All-terrain Wheelchairs* are designed for the more rugged, steeper trails, being able to cope with grass, mud, cobbles, rocky areas, steep slopes, steps, high kerbs, sand and even snow. That said, deep and dry powdery sand can be a problem and going out on steep snowy slopes is NOT recommended even when snow covers a recognised trail. This is because it is very likely to have become icy by other people compacting it.

I have tried to determine which type of wheelchair is suitable for each trail in the brief introductory paragraph before the main text. Obviously if a trail is suitable for manual chairs it is suitable for all other types as well.

Please note that the ultimate responsibility for undertaking each trail lies with the user. When using a battery operated wheelchair it is important to ensure that the battery is fully charged and is capable of doing the mileage required, with something to spare. Chairs with four-wheel drive are preferable for the rougher trails. Also a seat that tilts backwards for going downhill is also good. Steep uphill sections can be a problem where traction is poor. *However, if you are in any doubt whatsoever about the feasibility of any particular section ahead of you it is important to turn around and return to the car park.*

For the purpose of this guide it is presumed that wheelchair-bound people have a family member or a friend to accompany them during their outdoor experience. I believe it is important for everyone to interact with each other, making being outdoors a sociable occasion. I have also presumed, rightly or wrongly, that solo use is inadvisable on these trails. Ground clearance of at least 8 inches (20 cms) is needed for the rougher trails.

No stiles will be encountered but some gates need to be negotiated. These are mentioned in the text. Obviously with helpers that is no problem. It is important to realise that some of these trails, whilst executed fairly quickly by walkers, will often take longer and enough time should be allowed to complete the chosen trail, especially the longer ones. Mileages given are for return journeys, but no timings have been given.

It is important to wrap up warmly in winter, whilst in summer sun protection will be needed, as well as having a supply of drinking water. In winter it is prudent to take a warm drink because sitting down does not get the blood circulating. Winter clothing should entail three layers and a waterproof, as well as a woolly hat, scarf and gloves. Legs also need to be amply insulated. But the rewards are great and to feel the glow on ones face at the end of the day in a warm local pub or café is a wonderful feeling. *But always BEWARE of icy conditions.*

I hope this guide motivates wheelchair and scooter users to get out into the country. It highlights many possibilities for the enjoyment of this wonderful area. It would be greatly appreciated that if you have any issues with this guide to contact me via the publisher to make improvements for the next edition. I thank you in advance for that.

All that remains is for you to have fun – and I hope the sun shines for you!

WALK 1

ABER FALLS

DESCRIPTION Aber Falls (Rhaeadr Fawr) is one of the iconic waterfalls of Wales. The 2¾ miles trail is very pretty and rises gently with gradients of no more than 1:8 through a natural habitat of indigenous trees and plants. The total height gain is 100 feet on a trail around 5 feet wide. Soon after the start there is an exhibition of life through the ages and an interpretation centre. The smaller waterfall (Rhaeadr Fach) can also be seen along the trail to the main fall. There are information plaques at intermittent intervals. Ideally suited to off road scooters those who use manual wheelchairs will experience greater difficulty. However, with help they too will be able to get to the falls.

START From the upper, Natural Resources Wales, car park beyond Bont Newydd.

DIRECTIONS Turn off the A55 when travelling from the east or west along the A55 at junction 13 into the village of Abergwyngregyn. At the sign for the falls follow the narrow road up through the village to a parking area on the right very close to Bont Newydd. Drive over the bridge and continue until it is possible to turn left into the main car park. A small fee is payable but there is a disabled toilet here as well as others.

Go out of the car park back down the road towards the bridge to where it is possible to TURN LEFT to a wide usually padlocked black metal gate. Go through the amply wide kissing gate on the right of this and follow the track straight ahead passing to the right of a curious barrel shaped shelter. Pass through the wide gap to the right and continue gradually up the gravel track to the exhibition and interpretation centre. The track continues up and passes through a gate. A more or less level section continues through another gate. Keep following the track past a circle of stones and a standing stone. *Just before the track narrows there is a lovely view of Rhaeadr Fach over to right seen through a gap between the trees.* When the track narrows it rises again through the last of the gates. There is a lovely view of the fall from here.

Keep following the track, which for the last 50 yards is quite rough, to a superb level vantage point to view the waterfall. Return the same way to the car park.

Close to the falls an information board explains about the pile of stones to the right hand side of the path when going up. These are the remains of a round house built between 2,000 – 2,700 years ago. The standing stone in the pile of stones has been dated to approximately 2,000 BC.

Abergwyngregyn, *although small, is an interesting and a historically important little village. A large, grassy, circular mound is very prominent and is known as Llewelyn's Mound. However, it more than likely predated Llewelyn by over six hundred years being built around the 5th or 6thC and possibly above the body of a champion warrior.*

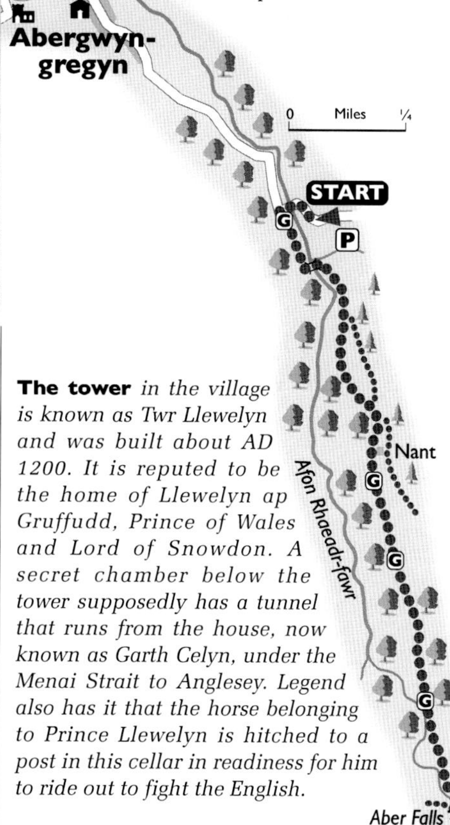

The tower *in the village is known as Twr Llewelyn and was built about AD 1200. It is reputed to be the home of Llewelyn ap Gruffudd, Prince of Wales and Lord of Snowdon. A secret chamber below the tower supposedly has a tunnel that runs from the house, now known as Garth Celyn, under the Menai Strait to Anglesey. Legend also has it that the horse belonging to Prince Llewelyn is hitched to a post in this cellar in readiness for him to ride out to fight the English.*

WALK 2

JANUS'S PATH

DESCRIPTION This is a pleasant ¼ mile suitable for an evening or break between rainstorms and ideal for manual wheelchairs. The trail has superb views across Llyn Cwellyn to the fine crag of Castell Cidwm nestling in a steep gully just above the lake. Mynydd Mawr, 2,290 feet (698 metres), is the towering mountain above. The trail predominantly consists of duck-boarding with a couple of very short compacted gravel sections.

START From the Snowdonia National Park car park opposite the Snowdon Ranger Youth Hostel.

DIRECTIONS From Beddgelert drive along the A4085 towards Caernarfon. Go through Rhyd Ddu and continue for almost 2 miles to the Snowdon Ranger Youth Hostel. Turn left almost opposite into the car park, which is free for disabled blue badge holders. There are toilets for all. Alternatively catch the S4 Sherpa Bus from Beddgelert or go on the Welsh Highland Railway to the Snowdon Ranger. When driving from the Caernarfon direction turn right off the A4085 almost opposite the Snowdon Ranger Youth Hostel.

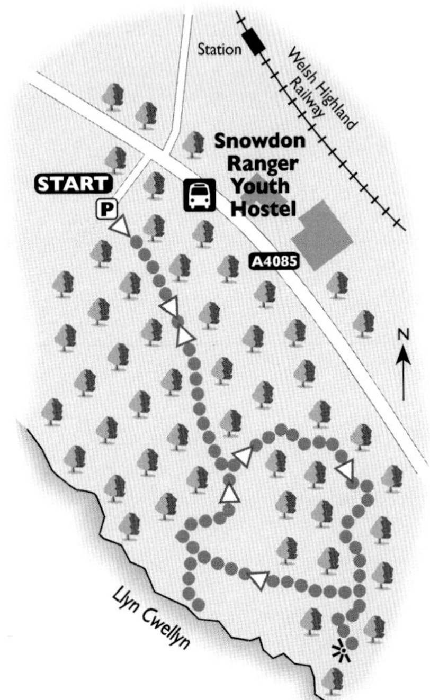

Go out of the car park past the payment machine. There is an information board on the left and a stone pillar on the right with a poem in Welsh and English on the right. However, there is a word of caution, albeit tongue in cheek, on the left here. A sign indicates that children under 100 need to be supervised!!

Continue along the gravel track to a footbridge Cross this and TURN LEFT at the junction just ahead. Continue slightly up and along to the next junction. Go straight ahead before curving right and down to a platform almost at the lake's edge. Continue to the next junction and TURN LEFT to a platform on the edge of the lake from where there are fine views of the lake and Mynydd Mawr. Return to the junction and TURN LEFT to the footbridge and back over it to the car park.

Janus *is a God with two faces. He can see this world and the other world at the same time. He symbolises change and transition and became known as the God of gates, bridges and forks in paths, places of barriers and choices.*

The legend of *Llyn Cwellyn concerns a young shepherd from Betws Garmon who fell hopelessly in love with a fairy who lived in the lake. In time she became his wife on the strict condition that he must not strike her with iron. If he was to do so she would disappear back into the other world to her people. For years all was well and they had two children. One day the couple were trying to catch a horse and the husband threw a bridle at it accidently hitting his wife on the cheek. Instantly his fairy wife disappeared into the lake never to be seen again, apart from one occasion when she appeared at her husbands' window late at night asking him to take good care of her children.*

The *120 feet (37 metres) deep Llyn Cwellyn covers an area of some 220 acres. It is one of the few lakes in Wales where Arctic Char may be found.*

WALK 3
LLYN Y GADAIR

DESCRIPTION This is a very scenic level 1¾ miles trail although there are gates, but life is made much easier with a helper to open these. The trail described is suitable for manual wheelchairs. There are some tremendous views of the surrounding mountains whilst the sound of the Welsh Highland Railway can be heard when it passes through Rhyd Ddu. With binoculars it is possible to see people atop Snowdon and the easily visible mountain railway chugging its way to the summit.

START From the Snowdonia National Park car park in Rhyd Ddu.

DIRECTIONS From Beddgelert drive along the A4085 towards Caernarfon. On entering Rhyd Ddu turn right into the Snowdonia National Park car park close to the station for the Welsh Highland Railway. Disabled parking is free and there are disabled toilets. Alternatively catch the S4 Sherpa Bus from Beddgelert or travel on the Welsh Highland Railway to Rhyd Ddu.

Go out of the car park and cross the road, CAREFULLY, to go through the ornate gate straight ahead onto the gravel path. Pass by an information board to a footbridge over a stream. Go through a wide gate and cross the bridge passing through the next gate 50 yards further. At the path junction there is a marker post, BEAR LEFT towards Llyn y Gadair.

Pass through a gate and follow the fenced path across the causeway.

Along *this there are fine views ahead of Mynydd Drws-y-coed 2,280 feet (695 metres) and to the right of this is Y Garn, 2,077 feet (633 metres) with a very steep right hand profile. Over to the left is Beddgelert's mountain, Moel Hebog 2,569 feet (783 metres). To the right of it is Moel yr Ogof 2,149 feet (655 metres) and Moel Lefn 2.093 feet (638 metres). Behind and to the right of Snowdon 3,560 feet (1,085 metres) is Yr Aran 2,451 feet (747 metres). To the left of Snowdon is Moel Cynghorion 2,211feet (674 metres).*

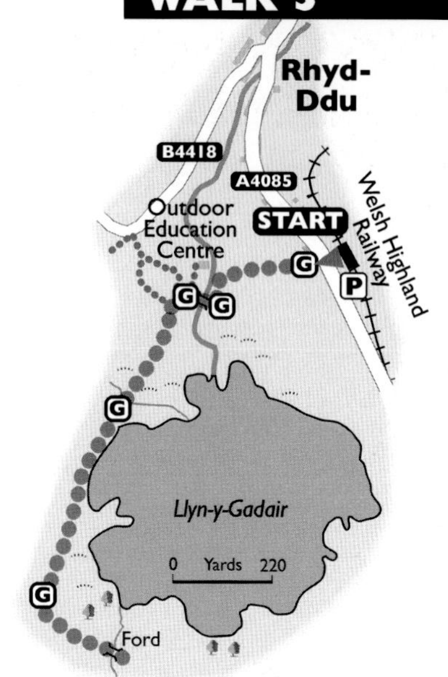

Go through the gate at the far end and continue to an information board on the left. Just beyond this TURN LEFT through the gate. Follow the path through old buildings of the Cadair Wyllt Slate Quarry. Continue for a couple of hundred metres passing several opportunities for picnics. It is best to turn round and reverse the outward journey back to the car park at the bridge by the side of a ford.

Llyn y Gadair *is a haunt of mischievous fairies, Tylwyth Teg, who dance by the lake at every full moon. One particular story about them concerns a young man returning to his farm one evening when he happened to meet the fairies dancing by the lakeside. Transfixed he stopped to watch but fell asleep waking to find that he was covered with gossamer. This made him invisible to the search parties who were looking for him. It was not until the following evening that he was released. Bemused, he wandered the slopes of Y Gadair totally unaware of where he was until dawn the following day when he realised he was only a mile from home!*

Ffridd Uchaf, *a nearby blanket bog, helps to reduce the impact of climate change by storing carbon and is a natural water filter acting as a water store during wet and dry periods.*

WALK 4

PEN-Y-PASS TO LLYN LLYDAW

DESCRIPTION This is an adventurous 3½ miles excursion into the heart of the Snowdon massif. The views are stupendous and it is well worth the effort to reach the lake where time can be spent admiring the fine conical form of the highest mountain in Wales and England. Manual wheelchairs will need a fair amount of help but scooters will manage the trail with little problem although I recommend that you have a companion.

START At Snowdonia National Park car park at Pen-y-pass.

DIRECTIONS The car park is reached easily from Llanberis on the A4086 but an early start is advisable as it is usually full by 08.00. There are disabled toilets at the car park, although there is only one dedicated disabled parking bay. Otherwise parking is available on the outskirts of Nant Peris in the pay and display car park for the park and ride bus service to Pen-y-pass. This is of course free to blue badge holders. Buses that operate this are wheelchair friendly. When travelling from the Beddgelert direction turn left off the A498 at the Pen-y-Gwryd onto the A4086 and from the Capel Curig direction follow the A4086 to where it turns right at the Pen-y-Gwryd to Pen-y-Pass.

Go through the gate at the far end of the car park opposite the entrance onto the Miner's Track. Follow the good track with increasingly good views down into the Gwynant Valley.

The Inn of the Sixth Happiness *was filmed in this valley as it was deemed to be a very close likeness to a Chinese valley.*

Pass the small but pretty Llyn Teyrn down to the left. *Note the ruins of the old miner's barracks close to the shore.* Keep following the rising path to where a pipeline, down to the left, comes close to the path.

The pipeline *delivers water from Llyn Llydaw to the Cwm Dyli hydro-electric power station in the Gwynant Valley, the oldest power station in Britain. It has supplied electricity to the National Grid since it was commissioned in 1906! It was built originally to supply an electric railway which was to run through the Gwynant Valley connecting with all slate quarries and mines. Fortunately the scheme came to nought when it ran out of funds. The pipeline is featured in the James Bond movie 'The World is Not Enough'. Llyn Llydaw is some 190 feet deep.*

Continuing, the views become increasingly dramatic.

Up to the left *is Lliwedd 2,946 feet (898 metres) whilst straight ahead is the fine conical shape of Snowdon 3,560 feet (1,085 metres). To the right is Crib y Ddysgl (sometimes known as Garnedd Ugain) 3,494 feet (1,065 metres) and finally up to the right is Crib Goch 3,028 feet (923 metres). The ridge running from Crib y Ddysgl to Crib Goch is known simply as the Crib Goch ridge and is an iconic, wonderful, but quite easy, scramble.*

Bear right at the fork in the path to reach the causeway across Llyn Llydaw, literally meaning 'Brittany Lake'.

The Miner's Track *was built to service the Britannia copper mine but this was not the original route that was used to get the copper out! In the beginning miners lugged the copper ore up 'Llwybr y Mul' (Mule's Path) to Bwlch Glas below the summit of Snowdon. It was then transported down the west side on a sledge pulled by two horses to Llyn Cwellyn before being taken by cart to Caernarfon.*

Prior to the building of the causeway horses pulled wagons full of copper ore from Britannia Mine and were ferried across the lake to shorten the journey down to Pen-y-pass. The causeway was built in 1853 after an accident in which a horse drowned. For it to be built the water level was lowered 12 feet. During this process a prehistoric 10 feet by 2 feet oak, dug-out, canoe was discovered! Mining ceased n 1916.

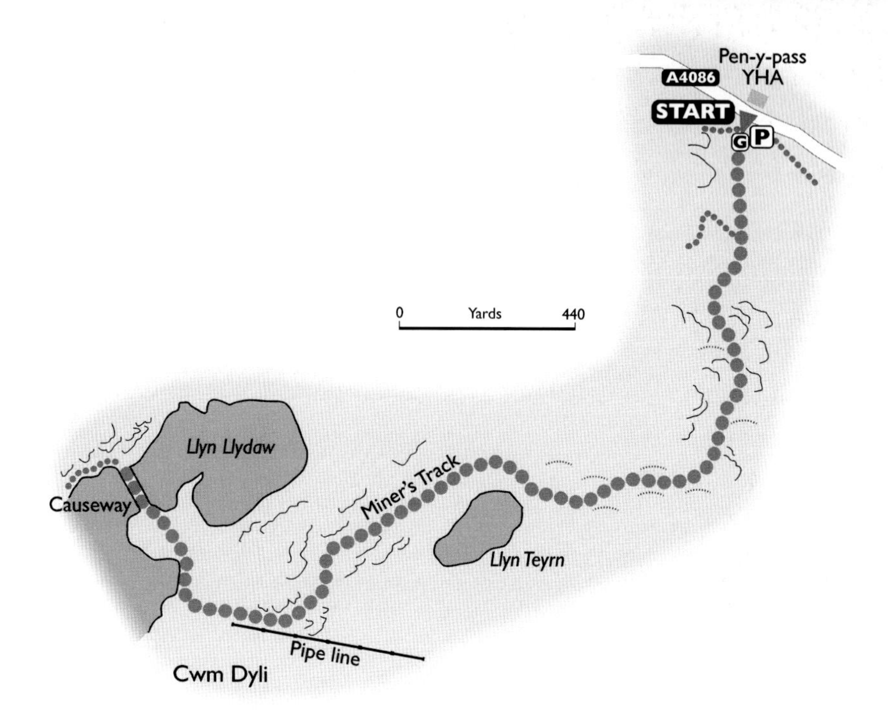

Llyn Teyrn and the Miner's Path on the way towards Llyn Llydaw

WALK 5

A VISIT TO THE HOUSE OF THE AUTHOR OF RUPERT BEAR

DESCRIPTION This is a pleasant ¾ mile mainly level journey to visit the home of the illustrator and writer of Rupert Bear stories, Alfred Edmeads Bestall MBE. It passes the very pretty terraced cottages of Tai Sygun before reaching 'Penlan' where Alfred lived for 30 years. This trail is suitable for manual wheelchairs but a push will be needed up the short rise to the house.

START From the main car park in Beddgelert close to the Welsh Highland Railway station.

DIRECTIONS The car park is found by turning off the A498 between the Royal Goat and the Tourist Information Centre. There are no toilets in the car park but parking is free for blue badge holders. There are three disabled bays.

Go out of the car park and TURN LEFT into the village. TURN RIGHT down a narrow lane before crossing the road bridge. Continue past Gwynneth Crafts, with the Afon Colwyn to the left. *Note the plaque to the film 'The Inn of the Sixth Happiness' on the wall to the right.* Continue past the toilets, the disabled one needs a RADAR key, to the footbridge spanning the combined flow of the Afon Colwyn and the Afon Glaslyn. Cross this. BEAR LEFT and then RIGHT immediately to walk on the gravel path to the right of the green in front of a very pretty row of terraced houses, Tai Sygun.

At the 'T' junction TURN LEFT and then RIGHT at the finger post up a narrow lane. The house, 'Penlan', is reached up a quite steep road 100 yards up on the left. Return to the finger post and continue straight ahead to a bridge. TURN LEFT immediately before it and follow the path by the side of the Afon Glaslyn downstream to the footbridge. TURN RIGHT over this to return to the car park.

Rupert Bear *was created by the English artist Mary Tourtel. The comic strip first appeared in the Daily Express on 8 November 1920. In 1935 the Rupert stories were taken over by Alfred. He was already an artist and storyteller. Born in Mandalay, Burma on 14th December 1892, he died on the 15th January 1986. Alfred lived in the house from 1956 to 1986. His first story was published on the 28th June 1935 and the last on the 22nd July 1965 although he still did covers for Rupert Annuals until 1973.*

The character Rupert Bear lives with his parents in a house in Nutwood, a fictional idyllic English village. He is depicted wearing a red sweater and bright yellow checked trousers, with matching yellow scarf. Usually seen as a white bear he was originally brown and was made white to save on printing costs.

The majority of the other characters in the series are also anthropomorphic animals (animals with humanoid forms). Regardless of species they are all drawn roughly the same size as Rupert referring to them as his 'chums' or 'pals'. His best friend was Bill Badger. Others were an elephant (Edward Trunk), a mouse (Willie), Pong-Ping the Pekingese, Algy Pug, Podgy Pig, Bingo the Brainy Pup, Freddie and Ferdy Fox and finally Ming the dragon.

Rupert was helped on many of his adventures by the kindly Wise Old Goat who also lives in Nutwood. The few main human characters in the stories were the Professor (who lives in a castle with his servant), Tiger Lily (a Chinese girl), and her father 'The Conjuror'. Perhaps Alfred's most famous drawing was 'The Frog's Chorus'. This inspired the cartoon video 'The Frog Song' composed by Sir Paul McCartney.

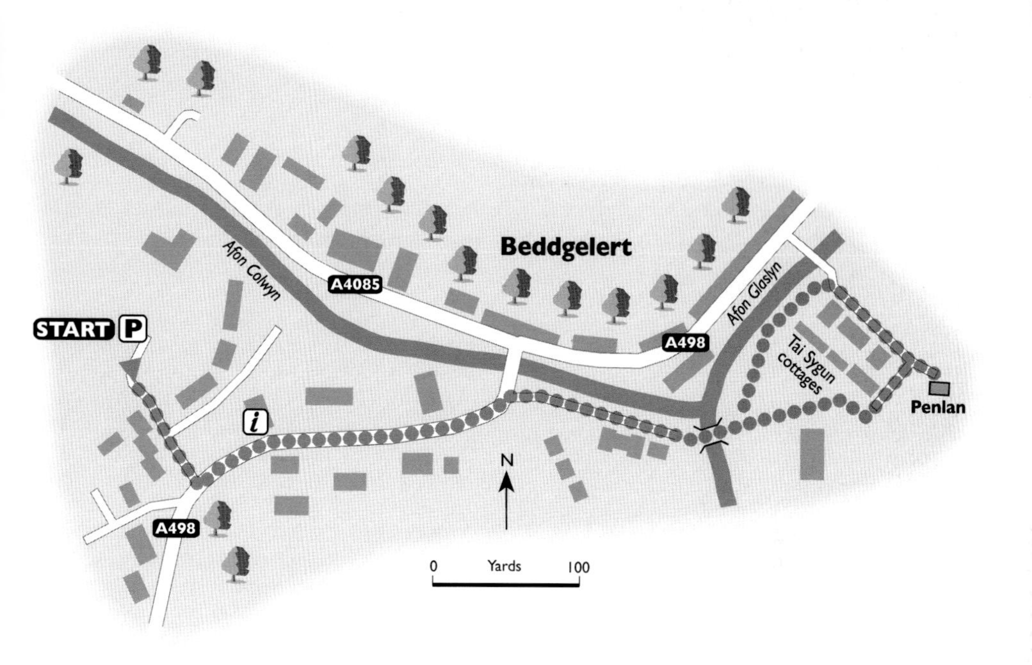

Tai Sygun cottages just beyond the footbridge close to the start

WALK 6

GELERT'S GRAVE & THE AFON GLASLYN

DESCRIPTION A lovely 1½ miles level trail either on a tarmac or concrete surface. Initially it goes alongside the Afon Colwyn and then the Afon Glaslyn to visit Gelert's Grave. After continuing downstream to the foot and railway bridges over the Afon Glaslyn the trail returns upstream to the village. This trail is suitable for manual wheelchairs. Having a helper will make life easier by opening the gates.
START From the main car park in Beddgelert close to the Welsh Highland Railway station.
DIRECTIONS The car park is found by turning off the A498 between the Royal Goat and the Tourist Information Centre. There are no toilets in the car park but parking is free for blue badge holders. There are three disabled bays.

Go out of the car park to the A498 and TURN LEFT into the village. TURN RIGHT down a narrow lane just before crossing the road bridge. Continue past Gwynneth Crafts, with the Afon Colwyn to the left. Note the plaque to the film 'The Inn of the Sixth Happiness' on the wall to the right. Go past the toilets, the disabled one needs a RADAR key, to the footbridge spanning the Afon Glaslyn. DO NOT cross but TURN RIGHT through the gate. There is also a sign for Gelert's Grave. Follow the concrete path downstream. TURN RIGHT at a junction with a path, again signed to Gelert's Grave, and follow it through a gate to reach the grave. From here continue ahead on the path to the ruined house on the right and where there is a brass dog! BEAR LEFT following the path back to the riverside. Although it is possible to return to the village from here trail continues to the right.

TURN RIGHT through the gate and continue alongside the river on the concrete path. Pass through a harp shaped gate. When reaching the Welsh Highland Railway go through the gate and cross the footbridge. If you are lucky there is the chance of seeing a train on the Welsh Highland Railway. TURN LEFT at the far side and walk upstream. Pass through a metal gate. To the right of this is a sheet metal carving of a railway engine. Continue and pass through another gate just before reaching the footbridge spanning the combined flow of the Afon Glaslyn and the Afon Colwyn. TURN LEFT over this to return to the car park.

Alternatively the walk can be extended by following Walk 5 from the bridge to where Alfred Bestall lived whilst writing his Rupert Bear stories before returning to the car park.

The legend of Gelert *is recounted many times and similar stories exist in other countries. Although the legend already existed it has been said that David Pritchard, the landlord of the Royal Goat Hotel, erected the headstone some 200 years ago. He did this to try and improve tourism in the area. It had the desired effect. Tourists flocked to see the grave. The legend is mentioned in a 1592 manuscript written by Sir John Wynne of Gwydir whilst the crest for the principality of Wales was once a greyhound in a cradle.*

Some 800 years ago *Prince Llewelyn set out on a hunting trip with his hounds and huntsman. His baby son and heir, was left asleep in his cradle at home. The servant girl looking after him was far from reliable. As soon as the hunting party had left she went off to meet her lover for a stroll along the river. Llewelyn had a favourite hound called Gelert and he was puzzled as to why he could not see him at the hunt. He presumed the hound had gone back home but a premonition that something dreadful had happened sent Llewelyn galloping home. On arriving he found the floor awash with blood and torn bedclothes. The cradle was empty and overturned. Gelert appeared with blood dripping from his mouth. Unfortunately for Gelert, Llewelyn acted on impulse and presuming the dog had killed his son he drew his sword in a rage and killed the hound. The dying howl from Gelert had a feeble echo, seemingly coming from under the bed-*

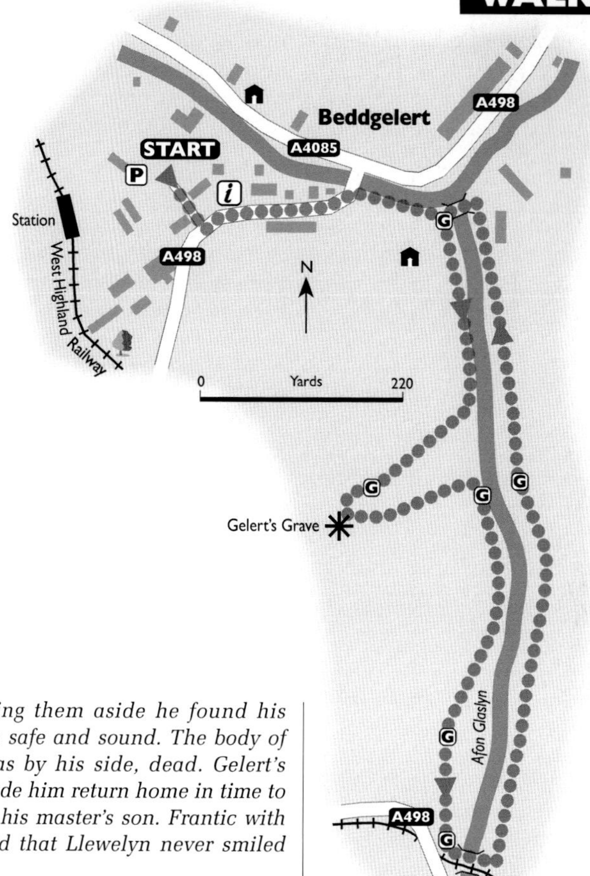

clothes. Dragging them aside he found his son underneath safe and sound. The body of a huge wolf was by his side, dead. Gelert's instinct had made him return home in time to save the life of his master's son. Frantic with sorrow it is said that Llewelyn never smiled again.

The Harp Gate on the Afon Glaslyn riverside path

WALK 7

THE KINGFISHER TRAIL & THE QUARRYMAN'S HOSPITAL

DESCRIPTION The short trails here are steeped in history and with superb views, not only of the remains of the old quarry workings but scenically too. The surface is firm and suitable for manual wheelchairs. The road to the quarry hospital is paved all the way and a visit is highly recommended. The final rise to the hospital is quite steep but negotiable by all, but with help for manual chair users. Most of the Slate Museum is accessible but help will be needed for some areas.

START All the trails start from the Gilfach Ddu car park at the National Slate Museum.

DIRECTIONS The car park is easily reached from Llanberis down the road almost opposite the Snowdon Mountain Railway. Parking for blue badge holders is free and there are disabled toilets here.

Trail 1 Go out of the car park and cross the Llanberis Lake Railway line. BEAR RIGHT and pass through the impressive slate bridge into Vivian Quarry. Note the 'Blondin' dangling over the lake. Continue to a viewing platform. It is possible that divers will be here as well as rock climbers. Return under the bridge.

Trail 2 For this trail TURN RIGHT on the return from Trail 1 after passing under the bridge keeping to the right of the Llanberis Lake Railway buildings. Continue along the grass/gravel track to the foot of the very impressive V2 incline. Return to the level crossing.

Trail 3 This trail visits the Quarryman's Hospital. Cross over the railway line and TURN LEFT to follow the wide pavement with the museum to the right. At the next level crossing cross the road and the lines and TURN LEFT up the road. There is a finger post with an accessible sign. The road rises gently and passes beneath an incline bridge. TURN LEFT 25 yards beyond this to view a twin track incline. This is the Garret Side Incline. Return to the road and TURN LEFT. Follow it up to a magnificent slate wall up to the right. Continue under the next incline bridge (for the V2 incline) dated 1886 to where the road rises somewhat more steeply. Where it becomes less steep, TURN LEFT into the hospital. There are superb views of Llyn Padarn from here. The hospital has an accessible ramp. Return to the car park.

Trail 4 At the far side of the car park opposite the entrance is a marker post and plaque to the right of it denoting the start of the Kingfisher Trail. TURN LEFT and follow a compacted gravel/grass track. TURN RIGHT at the second turning, the first has tree roots sticking up. Go along to a viewing platform after crossing a bridge. There is a good view of Llyn Padarn. The V2 incline is seen to the right as well as the Quarryman's Hospital. Behind is the fine form of Dolbadarn Castle.

Return to where a two way arrow is seen on a circular plaque and BEAR LEFT in front of it. Continue to a track. This leads down to the pleasure boat pier. TURN LEFT and follow the less wide track in front of the main track to where it ends close to the pier. There are commanding views of Lake Padarn and Llanberis from here. Return to the car park.

There is a leaflet obtainable in the information kiosk in the car park but below are some other interesting facts about the area.

The Quarryman's Hospital *has memorabilia from the 1800s and includes an operating theatre, an original X-Ray machine and what nowadays would be seen as gruesome operating instruments. There is selection of photographs of the quarrymen. Information plaques tell the story of some of the incidents and of life in the quarry.*

The Garret Side Incline *was the lowest of a series of inclines bringing slate down from higher in the huge quarries. The V2 incline was built in the 1860s and continued in service until the 1920s. The wagons had a level base and slates were loaded on to one of the wagons. The loaded wagon travelled down whilst the empty one went up. The incline was restored in 1998. The width of each track is 5 ft 6 inches with both having a gradient of 1:1.3.*

Blondins *are specialised forms of Chain Inclines. They allow loads to be picked up and transported and set down at any point along it.*

Slate *had many uses and apart from the obvious ones of slates for roofs and as building material – it was used for the beds for snooker tables, cosmetics , building roads, walls, fences, homeopathic remedies, gravestones and cisterns. All the best snooker tables have slate beds! Slate form the Llanberis quarries was exported worldwide.*

Llyn Padarn *is not particularly deep, having a maximum depth of only 100 feet. It is, however, the 6th deepest in Wales. It is home to the Arctic Char, a species of fish dating back to the last Ice Age.*

The Llanberis Lake Railway *has a track gauge of 1 ft 11½ inches along 2 miles of track along the shore of Llyn Padarn on part of the old track-bed of the slate railway to Port Dinorwic. One of the carriages has been adapted for disabled users.*

Although a dock *existed at Port Dinorwic a new dock was built at Port Dinorwic in 1828 when lime was extracted at Brynadda close by. The Assheton Smith family owned the Vaynol Estate and developed the Dinorwic Quarry in the late 18thC. Modern day Y Felinheli was once Port Dinorwic or alternatively Port Dinorwig.*

Quarrying *first took place in 1787 after a lease had been granted by Assheton Smith. Dinorwic Quarry was the second largest in the world only exceeded by its neighbour Penrhyn Quarry on the other side of hill at Bethesda. At its peak the quarry produced 100,000 tons and employed 3,000 men. Production ceased in 1969.*

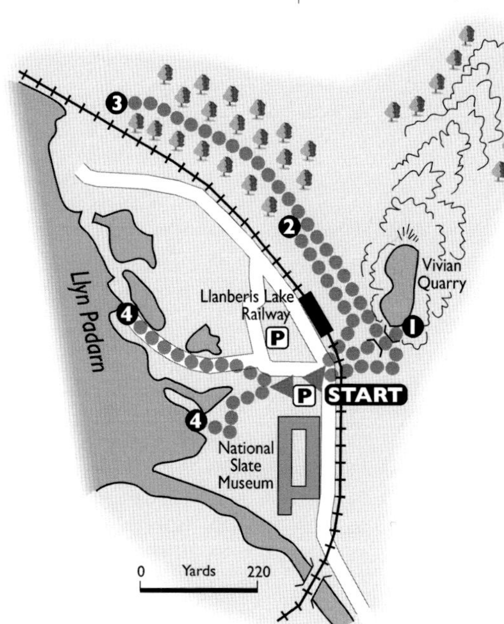

WALK 8

DOUGLAS FIRS & PUZZLE TRAIL, BETWS Y COED

DESCRIPTION A lovely half-a-mile, especially so on a summer evening, through mixed woodland. The animal puzzle trail is a great one for youngsters spotting and naming the 12 wildlife clues. The Douglas Firs are a magnificent sight alongside the tumbling Afon Llugwy. A leaflet for the animal puzzles can be obtained from Natural Resources Wales. This trail is suitable for manual wheelchairs.

START At the Gwynedd County Council, Pont y Pair car park in Betws y Coed.

DIRECTIONS From the A5 in Betws y Coed turn onto the B5106 that leads to Trefriw. Turn left immediately after crossing the bridge and then right into the car park. Parking is free if displaying a blue badge and parked in one of the six disabled parking bays. There are disabled toilets here.

Cross the road from the car park and TURN RIGHT to where the start of the walk will be found next to a finger post and information boards. Follow the gravel path onto a section of duckboards not far from the Afon Llugwy. At the 'Y' junction TURN RIGHT and go up to a track. TURN LEFT along this to where a gravel path can be followed to the left to reach a very fine picnic area close to the river. Follow the gravel trail to the 'Y' junction and BEAR RIGHT to return to the car park.

The Douglas Firs *were planted as young saplings in the 1920s. They now weigh over 10 tons each.*

Pont y Pair, *the Bridge of the Cauldron, was designed and partially built by Howell the mason from Bala. He died around 1475. It was around this feature that the village grew. In spate the cauldron effect is obvious. Traffic often grinds to a halt here as scores of people stare at the waterfalls and crashing water from the bridge.*

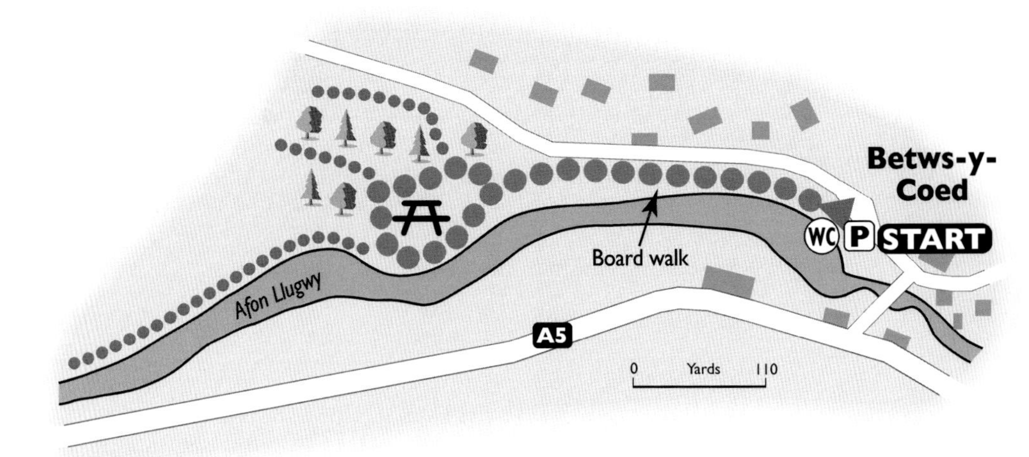

WALK 9

DOLMELYNLLYN ORNAMENTAL LAKE

DESCRIPTION This is a great place to observe wildlife. It is a small part of the Dolmelynllyn Estate and has been in the hands of the National Trust since 1936. The lake was created in the 19th century by damming the stream running through the woodlands. It is possible to see salmon and sea trout here as well as dragonflies. The half-a-mile long trail, although a little rough, is manageable by manual wheelchairs.

START Close to the lake and the estate houses on the edge of Ganllwyd.

DIRECTIONS Turn off the A470 towards Dolmelynllyn Hall by turning left just before entering the village of Ganllwyd and crossing the Afon Gamlan when travelling from the Dolgellau direction or, if coming from the north turn right just beyond the village. Continue up the access road for the Hall. When the road splits into three, the road straight ahead leads to the Hall. Below and to the left of the road the two other ways become tracks. Drive down the lowest one until just beyond the estate houses and park on the right, being careful not to block any tracks or buildings. It is important to display your blue badge.

From where your car is parked note the very fine beech trees in the field to the left. BEAR RIGHT from the car parking area and pass between fir trees to reach a 'Y' junction. TURN LEFT to reach the lake. Continue past two platforms with information boards and cross a footbridge. Keep following the path around the little lake over two more footbridges to a track junction. BEAR RIGHT and go over another footbridge and BEAR LEFT to return to the car parking area.

It is thought *that a building stood at Dolmelynllyn in medieval times but there is firm documentary evidence to show that a Tudor Manor House existed and parts of this are still in use today. The building passed through several gentry hands and became the focus of the Dolmelynllyn Estate. Various activities ranging from, for example, gold mining and experimental farming took place.*

Much of the building seen today is the result of a programme of enlargement carried out in Victorian times when it was owned by William Maddocks. Not only was he an MP and entrepreneur he was responsible for building the Cob at Porthmadog in 1811. Visitors included the poet Percy Bysshe Shelley during his brief holiday in Wales.

The lake was created some 250 years ago by Charles Raynolds Williams. He was also responsible for the layout of the gardens and parkland hereabouts. The stream is used by salmon returning to their spawning grounds.

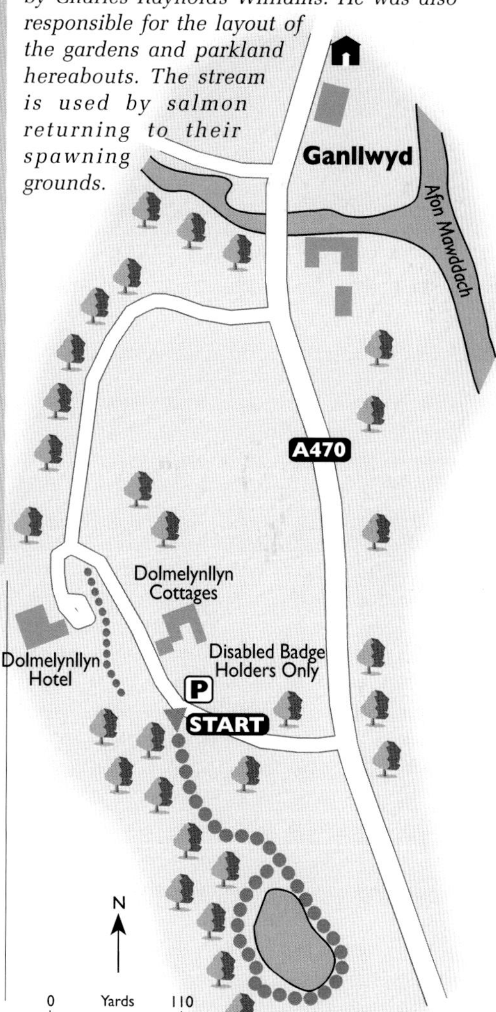

WALK 10

THE AFON EDEN

DESCRIPTION This is a pleasant and circular 1 mile trail down to the Afon Eden. It is also an animal puzzle trail needing some keen observation! It is great fun for all. A leaflet for this can be obtained from the Visitor Centre. After descending gradually to the river the trail follows the Afon Eden as it cascades and tumbles over rocks downstream of the fine road bridge to lovely picnic site. It is possible to continue the trail from this point by following the yellow markers back to the Visitor Centre. The trail is suitable for manual wheelchairs only as far as the picnic site and is only ½ mile. Scooter users will be able to continue on the circular trail. NOTE: This trail has six MP3 audio positions. The Place Tales App can be downloaded, for free on Android (4.0 and above) and iOS devices (iOS 7 and above), by accessing your wifi and typing in Natural Resources Wales. Go to Google Play Store or the Apple App store to download the right version for your device and select Place Tales. Phone network coverage is poor to non-existing locally. It is therefore more practical to download the App before your visit. Place Tales explain the natural and cultural heritage of the area.

START From the Natural Resources Wales Visitor Centre car park at Coed y Brenin.

DIRECTIONS From the south or north turn off the A470 at the obvious signed turning for the Coed y Brenin Visitor Centre. There are three disabled parking bays next to the Visitor Centre and three in the main body of the car park, but a blue badge must be shown to qualify for free parking. The accessible visitor centre is a good source for information as well as having a shop, café, running shop, bike shop and of course wonderful mountain biking. There are disabled toilets here.

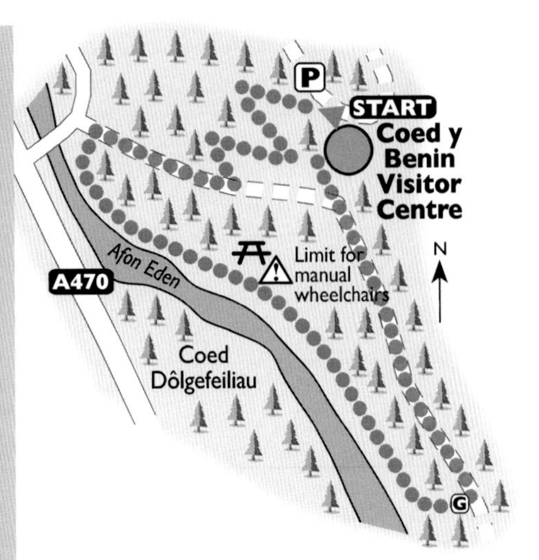

From the Visitor Centre follow the clearly marked Afon Eden trail that passes under the fine arch. Follow the blue arrows on the marker posts as it zigzags down and remembering to try and spot the animals from the clues given in the puzzle leaflet. Fun!

At the junction with a track, cross straight over keeping above the gate and follow the gravel path down to the RIGHT. The path makes a very sharp LEFT turn just before the next gate and continues down to the Afon Eden. Follow this, unfortunately quite short, but delightful path to a picnic site. For manual wheelchairs this is the turn round point. For those on scooters the following is a worthwhile addition.

Continue downstream from the picnic site on the good gravel path with the Afon Eden still to the right. Pass by a seat and start a very gradual ascent to a gate. Go through this to a track and TURN LEFT up it. At the obvious 'Y' junction, TURN RIGHT up the right arm of the 'Y' being aware that this is also used by bikers. Follow the narrower track to the Visitor Centre. Go up the ramp between the bike shop and the centre to the car park, perhaps via a drink and snack in the excellent café.

The area *was once a part of the ancient Nannau Estate that was founded in 1100 AD.by Cadougan, Prince of Powys. It was acquired in 1922 by the Forestry Commission (as Natural Resources Wales was known at that time). It is a working forest and as such it is important to heed any warnings seen on any of the trails.*

At one time this area of Coed y Brenin was known as Dolgefeiliau which translates to English as 'meadow of the smithies'. Near here a long time ago blacksmith's shops used to shoe cattle, pigs sheep and even geese in preparation for their long journey over the mountains to Smithfield and other markets in England.

WALK 11

GIANT DOUGLAS FIRS AT TY'N Y GROES

DESCRIPTION This is a half mile trail which gives everyone a chance to see these magnificent trees. The trail alongside the tumbling Afon Mawddach is delightful with many birds darting here and there. The trail can be completed in manual wheelchairs. NOTE This trail has 6 MP3 audio positions. The Place Tales App can be downloaded, for free on Android (4.0 and above) and iOS devices (iOS 7 and above), by accessing your wifi and typing in Natural Resources Wales. Go to Google Play Store or the Apple App store to download the right version for your device and select Place Tales. Phone network coverage is poor to non-existing locally. It is therefore more practical to download the App before your visit. Place Tales explain the natural and cultural heritage of the area.

START At the Natural Resources Wales car park Ty'n y Groes.

DIRECTIONS From Dolgellau follow the A470 towards Betws y Coed. Pass the Ty'n y Groes hotel on the left and turn right at the brown sign indicating Ty'n y Groes. The turning is also marked to Llanfachreth. Drive over the bridge crossing the Afon Mawddach and turn left immediately beyond it into the car park. There are disabled toilets here. When coming from the north on the A470 drive through Ganllwyd and turn left at the brown sign for Ty'n y Groes and Llanfachreth and continue to the car park.

Go out of the car park past the toilets and cross the road. Follow the gravel river side path past picnic tables to an information panel. Continue along the path passing through enormous trees, the tallest in Coed y Brenin, dubbed 'The King's Guardians'. The path splits so follow the RIGHT arm alongside the river. There is an interesting 'viewing bed' just before the split where you can lay down with help to view the canopy high above.

The path continues close to the Mawddach giving good views of it to reach a seat with a crown! By this is the largest of all the trees here and has been named 'The King'. Continue to a path junction. This is the point where the all ability trail ends. TURN LEFT back to return to the car park on a loop.

However, from the path junction beyond 'The King', it is possible with help to continue up to the tallest tree in the forest 'The Champion' and a viewing area of the river. Turn around here to return to the car park via the loop.

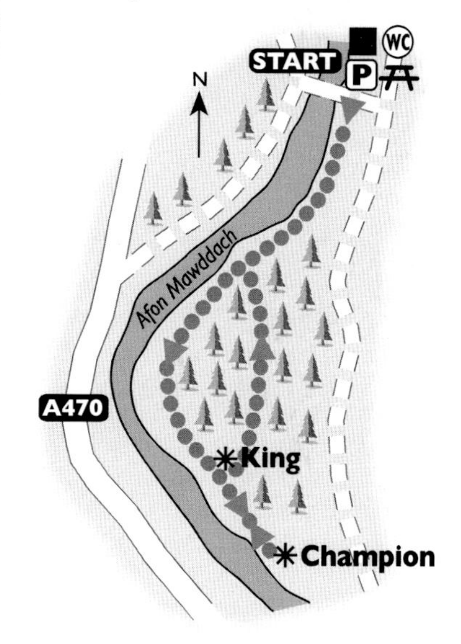

The Douglas Fir *(Pseudotsuga Menziesii) was discovered in 1791 in North America's Rocky Mountains by Archibald Menzies. The Scottish explorer, David Douglas sent the first seed back to Britain in 1827. The widest tree in the forest is known as 'The King' and measures 148 feet (45 metres) high, with a diameter of 39 inches (100 cm) whilst the tallest is 'The Champion', at 161 feet (49 metres) with a diameter of 32 inches (80 cm).*

WALK 12

WATERFALLS & GOLD MINE TRAIL

DESCRIPTION Although the track is somewhat rough on this 2¼ mile circular journey through the forest, the waterfalls are well worth the effort to see them. Mostly level there are some lovely views of the Afon Mawddach as it tumbles down its boulder bed on its journey to the sea, along with those from the footbridge close to the end of the trail. There are however, very short sections of slightly steeper and rougher track near the start but these are negotiable with care and, perhaps, some help for manual wheelchairs. *This trail is only suitable for manual wheelchairs as far as the bridge over the Afon Cain to view the fine Pistyll Cain, making it a 1¾ miles journey. All terrain wheelchairs will easily negotiate the remaining part of the trail.* NOTE: This trail has 8 MP3 audio positions. The Place Tales App can be downloaded, for free on Android (4.0 and above) and iOS devices (iOS 7 and above), by accessing your wifi and typing in Natural Resources Wales. Go to Google Play Store or the Apple App store to download the right version for your device and select Place Tales. Phone network coverage is poor to non-existing locally. It is therefore more practical to download the App before your visit. Place Tales explain the natural and cultural heritage of the area.

START At the Tyddyn Gwladys car park in Coed y Brenin.

DIRECTIONS When travelling north from Dolgellau on the A470 turn right by the 40 mph restriction sign at the far side of Ganllwyd onto the dead end minor road. From the north and travelling south on the A470, turn left at the 30 mph sign just before entering Ganllwyd. Follow this narrow road up to the small car park on the right. There are picnic tables, a lovely place to have a picnic after wards.

1 Go out of the car park and TURN RIGHT up the road. Where the tarmac ends go through the gate marked for Ferndale. Follow the quite rough track to a barrier by Ferndale. This is often locked but it is possible, with care, to go around it to the left. Follow the level track to cross a very short rougher section and where it briefly rises. *Just after the track levels again there is a great view of Rhaeadr Mawddach to the right. The remains of the old gunpowder works can be seen up to the left.* Continue to the bridge spanning the Afon Cain. There is a superb view of Pistyll Cain from this. This is where manual wheelchair users need to turn back making a 1¾ miles journey. Just beyond the bridge down the track to the right are the remains of the Gwynfynydd gold mine.

Gold was discovered *here in 1863 and produced gold until 1998 finally closing in 1999 due to Health and Safety issues. Over its life the mine produced some 45,000 troy ounces of high quality gold since 1884. It is interesting to note that the Queen was presented with a kilogramme of Welsh gold on her 60th birthday in April 1986 from here. Gold mined from here has been incorporated into the prestigious Glyndwr Award, a medal that has been awarded annually since 1995 for excellence in the arts of Wales by the Machynlleth Tabernacl Trust. The first recipient was the artist Sir Kyffin Williams.*

The land surrounding the mine was owned by Welsh Gold plc but Clogau Gold of Wales purchased around 80 acres of land surrounding the mine in mid-2013.Clogau gold mine is to be found high above Bontddu, a village by the side of the Afon Mawddach midway between Dolgellau and Barmouth. This mine produced 78,507 troy ounces of gold between 1862 and 1911. The mine was re-opened again 1989.

The mine is now to become the first rurally sensitive hydro scheme generating electricity for the local area. However, in the long term Clogau Gold will possibly look at mining again as another source of Welsh gold.

2 Continue along the track BEARING LEFT and up to a finger post at a track junction. TURN RIGHT and go over the bridge and over another short rougher section. Follow the track as it rises gently to a final rough section up to where the track levels at junction of tracks. BEAR RIGHT through a gap to the right of a gate and continue easily and much more smoothly gradually downhill to a level section before going up to a 'Y' junction.

3 BEAR RIGHT and descend slightly to another level section. Pass by some steps up to the left to reach a marker post 250 yards ahead by another track junction. TURN RIGHT very sharply almost doubling back on to a narrower but smooth track. Follow this and go around a hairpin bend to reach a bridge over the Afon Mawddach. Cross this but stop midway to admire the fine river scenery upstream of the river cascading down three small cataracts. Zigzag up the track at the far side to a 'Y' junction. Either go up to the LEFT to the road and TURN RIGHT up it to return to the car park, or, BEAR RIGHT at the junction and follow the narrow track back to the car park.

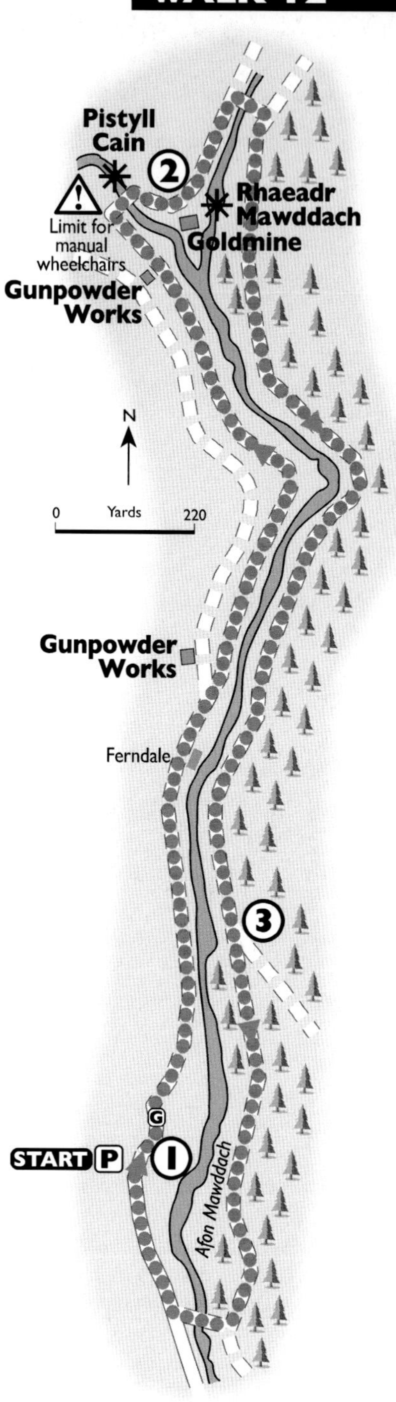

About the author

Des Marshall has had a lifelong interest in mountaineering, climbing, walking, canyoning and caving. As well as being an advisor, trainer and assessor in outdoor activities, he has undertaken many expeditions worldwide but now focuses more on local excursions. After moving away a few years ago, the lure of the plethora of exciting walking and climbing in Wales became too much and he now lives in Morfa Nefyn on the Llŷn peninsula.

WALK 13

TO GLASDIR COPPER MINE

DESCRIPTION This scenic half-a-mile trail is high above the gorge, with the Afon Babi tumbling through it, to end up at a viewpoint above the mine. From here there is also a wonderful view of Y Garn 2,063 feet (629 metres), an outlying peak of the Rhinogau. This trail is a great one for manual wheelchair users. NOTE: This trail has five MP3 audio positions. These are numbered 1, 2, 6, 7 and 8. The Place Tales app can be downloaded, for free on Android (4.0 and above) and iOS devices (iOS 7 and above), by accessing your wifi and typing in Natural Resources Wales. Go to Google Play Store or the Apple App store to download the right version for your device and select Place Tales. Phone network coverage is poor to non-existing locally. It is therefore more practical to download the App before your visit. Place Tales explain the natural and cultural heritage of the area.

START From the small disabled only car park at Pont Llam yr Ewig. There is room for two cars! There is also a picnic table here.

DIRECTIONS From Dolgellau follow the A470 towards Betws y Coed. Pass the Ty'n y Groes hotel and continue to the sign for Llanfachreth and the brown sign for Ty'n y Groes. Turn right here down this road and drive over the bridge crossing the Afon Mawddach passing the Ty'n y Groes car park to where the tarmac road bends to the right. Continue through the forest on the narrow road and at the next junction keep straight ahead going around a sharp bend. At the next junction turn up to the left and continue to a complex of junctions. Keep right at these and continue to the car park, on the right, immediately beyond the bridge spanning the Afon Babi. When coming from the north on the A470 drive through Ganllwyd and turn left at the brown sign for Ty'n y Groes and Llanfachreth. Continue down the road over the Afon Mawddach and follow the directions above from the Ty'n y Groes car park.

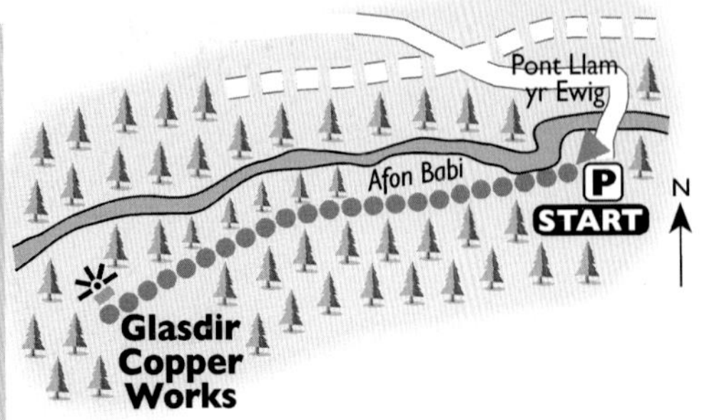

From the car park follow the level, gravel trail along an old tramway, admiring the fine views as you go.

Pont Llam yr Ewig *translates as the 'Bridge of the Hind's Leap'. Local folklore says that a fairy baby was exchanged for a local farmer's child!*

Glasdir mine *was one of the most extensive mines in the Dolgellau area. It was first opened around 1852 as a quarry. Between 1872 and 1913 some 13,077 tons of dressed copper left the mine. In 1907 the mine was fortunate to have a mill using the Elmore Flotation Process. The process was brought here by Stanley Elmore the owner of the mine had previously constructed the process at the Sygun Copper Mine but when the mine stopped working he transferred all the equipment to Glasdir. The mine finally closed in 1915. In terms of precious metals the mine produced 8,275 ounces of silver and 735 ounces of gold between 1872 and 1915.*

The flotation process entails using the waste material and water. This waste usually has some 1–2% of copper ore and is crushed. Water is then added and fed into a ball mill. This is a rotating drum with steel balls that crush the ore into a fine powder and forms slurry. When this is comes out of the mill it is fed into a rake classifier and then into flotation cells. Any particles that are too large are returned to the mill. Air is injected into the flotation cells where foaming agents are added. This creates froth and copper particles, because of their light weight, become a part of this froth. Heavier particles such as iron sink. The mixture of copper and froth containing around 20–40% copper continues for further processing to extract the copper itself.

WALK 14

TREE DISCOVERY TRAIL & THE AFON BABI

DESCRIPTION This quarter-of-a-mile trail is another great one for manual wheelchair users. However, for those with scooters an extension is possible. Many of the trees passed are labelled and are from different parts of the world. The Afon Babi is very pretty and the trail ends overlooking the ivy festooned Pont Llam yr Ewig. At the viewpoint is a wind up box telling a local folk story. Information about the trees can be obtained by the 'signal' posts that are passed on the journey.

START From the small disabled only Forest Garden car park. There are also picnic tables here.

DIRECTIONS From Dolgellau follow the A470 towards Betws y Coed. Pass the Ty'n y Groes hotel and continue to the sign for Llanfachreth and the brown sign for Ty'n y Groes. Turn right here down this road and drive over the bridge crossing the Afon Mawddach passing the Ty'n y Groes car park to where the tarmac road bends to the right. Continue through the forest on the narrow road and at the next junction keep straight ahead going around a sharp bend. At the next junction turn up to the left and continue to a complex of junctions. Keep right at these and continue to the car park, on the left 150 yards past the Pont Llam yr Ewig car park. When coming from the north on the A470 drive through Ganllwyd and turn left at the brown sign for Ty'n y Groes and Llanfachreth. Continue down the road over the Afon Mawddach and follow the directions from Ty'n y Groes car park.

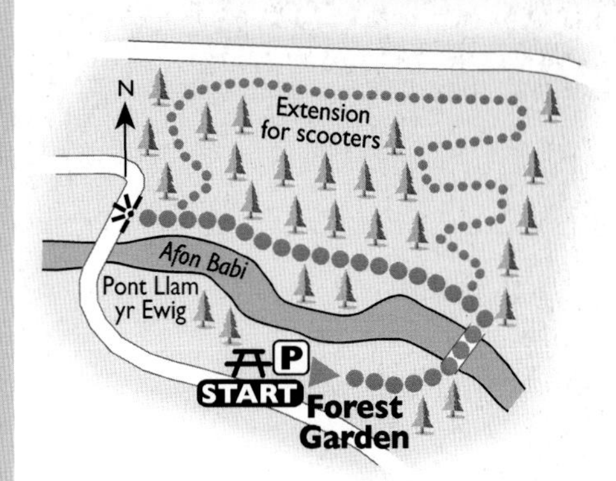

From the car park follow the trail crossing the footbridge over the Afon Babi to the end of the trail at the viewpoint. Use the push out 'signals' to learn about the trees. *Some of these are: Kashmir Birch; Douglas Fir Raoul, a type of beech; Siberian Spruce; Noble Fir; Lawson Cypress and Japanese Red Cedar.*

Pont Llam yr Ewig *translates as the 'Bridge of the Hind's Leap'. Local folklore says that a fairy baby was exchanged for a local farmer's child!*

An extension is possible for those using scooters by following the green markers. From the viewpoint TURN LEFT sharply at the marker post and zigzag up the gentle rise around five bends to a gate over to the left. BEAR RIGHT here and follow the level trail to reach a seat on the left at a 'Y' junction. Go down the right arm of the 'Y' and pass by a 'wind up' information post. This relates the story about 'The Demons Hollow Tree'. Zigzag down to the trail travelled earlier and TURN LEFT back over the footbridge back to your car. *Some of the trees seen on this journey are: Western Hemlock, Smooth Japanese Maple, Tulip Tree, Service Tree, Grand Fir, Wellingtonia and Scots Pine.*

WALK 15

FOEL ISPRI

DESCRIPTION The views from this half-a-mile trail are truly spectacular. It is ideal for manual wheelchairs. The Afon Mawddach can be seen meandering towards the amazing estuary with views down to Penmaenpool and Dolgellau. The impressive Cadair Idris massif is a splendid backdrop. This is a trail not to miss. The only drawback is that it is short. One other but very slight drawback is the drive up the very narrow road to the car parking area. It is important to have a helper as there are a couple of gates to open during the drive. The drive in itself is also a very pretty. There is a guard rail along the exposed path to avoid running off the trail!

START From a small car park close to a finely situated house Foel Ispri-uchaf.

DIRECTIONS Turn off the A496 when travelling from Dolgellau or Barmouth immediately opposite the turning to the toll bridge leading to Penmaenpool. Follow the narrow road steeply up to where it splits just after crossing a small bridge spanning a stream. Turn right here and continue up the narrower road to where a sign can be seen ahead for Cesailgwm Fawr. Turn right again just before this down the very narrow road driving past an accessible marker post for the 'New Precipice Walk'. Drive through a gate just beyond this and continue up the very pretty road through two more gates. The small car park is on the left immediately after the second gate and before reaching the house. Please park to allow others to use the car parking area.

Go along the good track towards the house. Note the old water wheel on the side of the house. BEAR RIGHT at the finger post and accessible sign by the 'Y' junction. Go through the gate and continue with increasingly dramatic views to go through another gate. Continue up a very gradual rise past a picnic table – indeed one of the most finely situated picnic tables anywhere!

There is a superb view *of Cadair Idris 2,930 feet (893 metres) and the satellite peak of Cyfrwy 2,661 feet (811 metres) to the right whilst further right again is Tyrrau Mawr 2,169 feet (661 metres). Down on the valley floor the Afon Mawddach meanders lazily towards its estuary. Dolgellau can be seen and the toll bridge at Penmaenpool.*

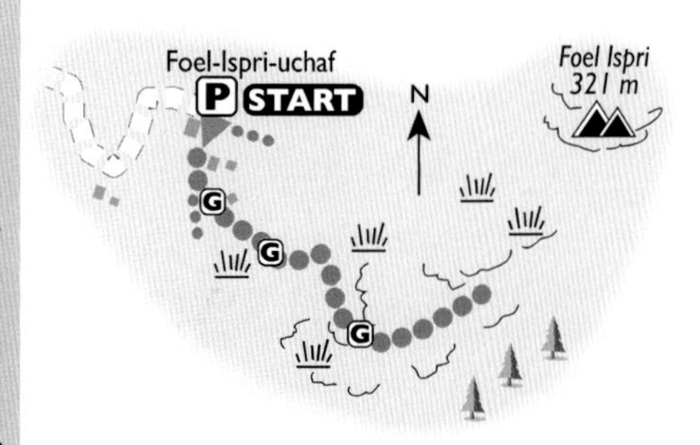

Go through another gate and past three seats. The trail unfortunately ends 25 yards past the last seat where the guard rail ends at a marker post. It is well worth taking a picnic to have at the picnic table on the return to the car park.

WALK 16

MAWDDACH TRAIL Dolgellau to Pont y Wernddu

DESCRIPTION Dolgellau is the eastern start for the Mawddach Trail. This and the next four descriptions make up the trail apart from the 1 mile section from Arthog to Morfa Mawddach as this is not very interesting. However, a trail exploring the Arthog Nature Reserve starting at Morfa Mawddach is included in walk 21. Starting from Dolgellau the 2 mile trail, suitable for manual wheelchairs, starts off, not by following the Afon Mawddach as might be expected, but by following the Afon Wnion! This river is followed all the way down to Pont y Wernddu and gives great views of Cadair Idris 2,930 feet (893 metres) towering above the town. The mountain is reputed to be the chair of a legendary giant called Idris. It is also said that if anyone spent the night on the mountain they would return a poet or a madman. There are many places in Wales where a similar story exists. The return journey is 2 miles.

START At the Gwynedd County Council main car park in Dolgellau close to Bont Fawr spanning the Wnion. Parking is free for disabled blue badge holders and there are also disabled toilets. There are 3 dedicated disabled parking bays.

Dolgellau *means 'Meadows of the Cells' in English which perhaps pertains to the many sheep pens in the area. Prior to 1283 when the town became known as 'Dolgethly', it was known as 'Dolkelew'. Owain Glyndŵr who had a Parliament in Machynlleth from 1402 held an assembly in the town in 1404 on the site of T H Roberts shop. It became the main town of the old county of Merioneth in the 16thC. During the 18th and 19thC Dolgellau had a large woollen industry specialsing in flannel, as did Machynlleth, that was used for soldier's uniforms. The town has perhaps the highest proportion of listed buildings of anywhere in Wales, with over 200. It became a conservation area in 1991.*

Bont Fawr *seen just upstream at the start of the start of the trail once had 10 arches when it was built in 1638. Three were, unfortunately, lost when the railway was built. A local folk story says that a fairy once lived in a pool under the bridge. After she married Hugh Evans, a local man, she told him not to follow her. One night frustrated as to where she went he followed her and in stalking her he fell and broke his leg. His wife tended him until he was able to walk again and then vanished forever!*

The trail is signed at the far (river) side of the car park. Turn left down the wide track and continue downstream with the rugby field to the left. The trail is briefly tarmacked but quickly becomes compacted gravel after the information board. Continue to the footbridge over the Afon Wnion and cross this. TURN LEFT at the sign for Barmouth immediately after the end of the bridge. DO NOT go through the tunnel under the road.

This is the start *of the track-bed of the railway. The line had reached Penmaenpool in 1865, having been built by Great Western Railway, but it was not until 1868 that the line from Bala reached the town. This had been constructed by Cambrian Railways. There were two stations in Dolgellau maintained by the two companies! In 1922 GWR took over the whole line. Steam trains operated throughout the life of the line that closed with Dr Beeching's axe in 1965. Fortunately the Snowdonia National Park had the foresight to purchase the line and converted it into a wonderful journey for all to enjoy whether cycling, walking, wheelchair bound or even riding a horse.*

Follow the trail now with the Afon Wnion on the left. *The fine, large building across the road to the right is the college.* This section of trail ends at the A493 with Pont y Wernddu to the left. The Pont y Wernddu car park is on the opposite side of the road alightly to the right. Either return to Dolgellau from here or continue along the next section to Penmaenpool by crossing the road and following the route as described in Walk 17.

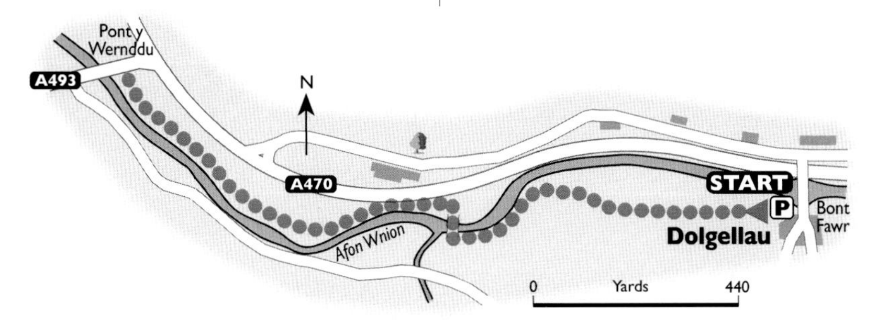

WALK 17

MAWDDACH TRAIL
Pont y Wernddu to Penmaenpool

DESCRIPTION Although this second section of the trail, suitable for manual wheelchairs, is only 2½ miles it leaves the Afon Wnion to reach the Afon Mawddach. On the way reed beds in the marshy fields either side of the trail are passed. These beds, one of the largest in Wales, are an SSI (Site of Scientific Interest). At one time they provided thatch for local houses. The habitat is a very important for a number of rare plants, birds and animals. Kingfishers are often spotted here.

START At the Snowdonia National Park car park at Pont y Wernddu.

DIRECTIONS When travelling from the north along the A470 turn right at the junction for the A493 to Tywyn before Dollgellau. Coming from the south it is better to keep on the bypass for Dolgellau and turn left onto the A493. The car park is almost immediately on the right of the road down a slight dip. There are no toilets of any kind here but there are some at Penmaenpool.

Go out of the car park, away from the road, passing an information board. Pass through the gate to the right of the cattle grid and follow the tarmac trail. Cross the old rail bridge spanning the Afon Wnion. Just beyond the bridge go through the obvious turning area and continue down the pretty tree lined trail to carefully cross a farm access road. Continue along the now open trail to the car park at Penmaenpool.

The George III hotel can be seen ahead and if drinks are needed carefully cross the toll road noting the wooden deck of the toll bridge to the right. BEWARE of the speed humps on the trail past the hotel as there is a slight risk of grounding.

Either return to Pont y Wernddu, or continue along the longer third section described in Walk 18.

Five years *prior to the railway arriving in 1865 Penmaenpool was an estate village. It had a row of terraced cottages serving a model farm which in turn served Penmaenucha Hall. This was the country residence of a Bolton cotton magnate. Before the railway ship building flourished. Interestingly, ships were launched sideways into the circular 'pool' by drink fuelled locals who had been plied with free booze.*

The George III *dates back to circa 1650. It was in two halves at that time with one half being a pub and the other a ship's chandlers for the thriving ship building industry. Around 1890 the two halves were joined to form the hotel. The lodge, a Victorian building, was erected to form a waiting room, ticket office and the station master's house for the adjacent station by Cambrian Railways, the original owner of the line before being taken over by Great Western Railway in 1922. The line closed in 1965 courtesy of Dr Beeching's axe! Gerald Manley Hopkins is reputed to have written a poem in one of the old guest books.*

The wooden decked *toll bridge was opened in 1879. Prior to this a ferry operated, certainly as far back as the 16thC. In 1966 the 'Prince of Wales' ferry from Barmouth capsized having hit the bridge. Passengers were flung into the river in to a fast incoming tide drowning 15 people. Staff from the hotel rescued 20 people using small clinker built boats.*

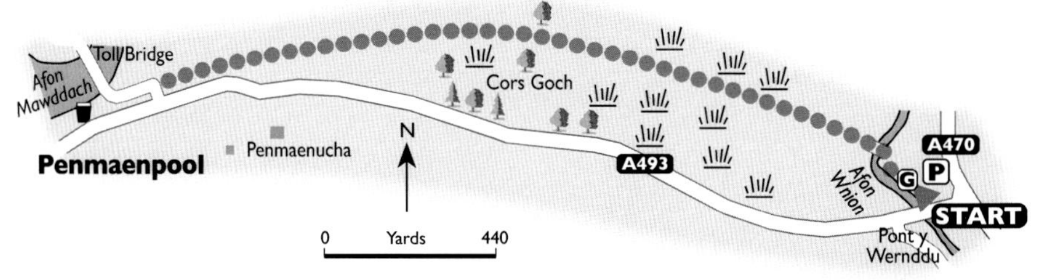

WALK 18

MAWDDACH TRAIL

Penmaenpool to Abergwynant Creek

DESCRIPTION This 5 mile section now starts to follow the Afon Mawddach and the estuary. It is a pretty journey with much to see and is suitable for manual wheelchair users. There are great views across the estuary towards Bontddu with the Rhinogau forming a wonderful backdrop. The section ends at Abergwynant where the Gwynant is spanned by a substantial bridge.

START At the Snowdonia National Park car park at Penmaenpool.

DIRECTIONS From Dolgellau follow the A493 to where it is possible to turn right towards the toll bridge. The car park is immediately before this on the right. From the south follow the A493 north to where a left turn leads to the car park and toll bridge. There are two disabled parking bays. Parking is free for all and there are disabled toilets here.

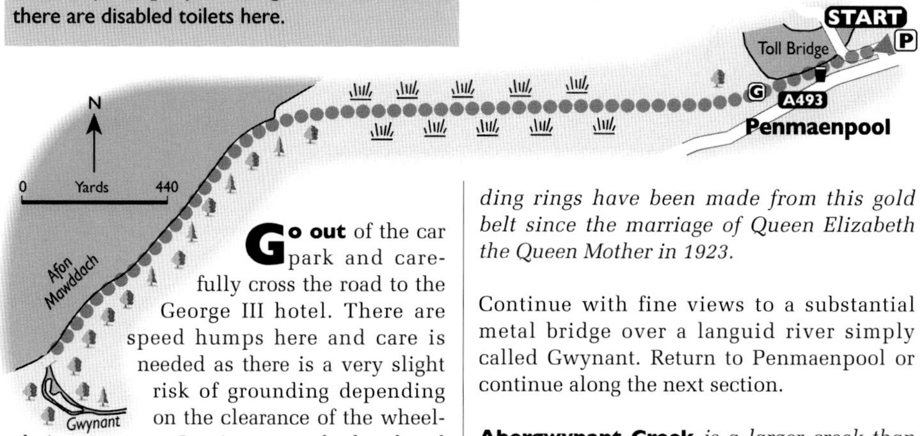

Go out of the car park and carefully cross the road to the George III hotel. There are speed humps here and care is needed as there is a very slight risk of grounding depending on the clearance of the wheelchair or scooter. Continue past the hotel and the houses to go through a gate by the last one. The trail continues and passes by a 'Length or Line's Man hut'.

This hut *built from railway sleepers has a brick fireplace, hearth and chimney. In times past track maintenance work was carried out by Length Men or Line Men. Great pride was taken to look after their length of track which could be anything from a few hundred yards of a complex line system or several miles of single track rail lines. Trains were always hauled by steam engines so to try and avoid the possibility of fire from engine sparks, Length Men cut the grass and bushes back from the line edge.*

As the trail *finally meets the estuary the buildings seen opposite are in the village of Bontddu. The most obvious of these is the dark, brooding one has a more modern white conservatory attached. It was built in 1873 and Neville Chamberlain was apparently a regular visitor. After the war ended in 1945 it was bought by Bill Hall, a decorated soldier. He converted it into a hotel subsequently running it for 40 years until his retirement in 1985. The hotel finally closed in 2000.*

Above the village *is the Clogau gold mine. A lode runs from Barmouth to Coed y Brenin. Many mines were started along this lode but only two had any measure of success. These were the Clogau and Gwynfynydd ones. See notes on Gwynfynydd in Walk 12. Royal wedding rings have been made from this gold belt since the marriage of Queen Elizabeth the Queen Mother in 1923.*

Continue with fine views to a substantial metal bridge over a languid river simply called Gwynant. Return to Penmaenpool or continue along the next section.

Abergwynant Creek *is a larger creek than most along the trail but each had their own ship building business. Between 1750 and 1865 around 318 ships were built along the Mawddach.*

WALK 19

MAWDDACH TRAIL
Arthog to Abergwynant Creek

DESCRIPTION This 5¾ mile section almost entirely follows the Afon Mawddach and estuary. Views are absolutely wonderful both up and downstream as well as across the river to the Rhinogau forming the skyline. This is suitable for manual wheelchairs.

START At the small Snowdonia National Park car park at Arthog next to the trail.

DIRECTIONS Follow the A493 from either the Dolgellau or Tywyn directions. At Arthog turn down the narrow access road to the car park. This turning is marked by a black tin shed on the left of the narrow road just after the turn down. It is easy to miss this turn. From the Tywyn direction this turning is just over 1 mile beyond the turning for Morfa Mawddach rail station. From the Dolgellau direction this is just after the village. Having turned, drive through a gate and continue along the road to the trail. Just before this go through a gate on the left into the car park. There are no facilities here but it is free for all and there is a picnic table.

Return out of the car park through the gate just driven through and TURN LEFT through another gate onto the Mawddach Trail. TURN RIGHT along this through yet another gate. Continue along the trail to some square blocks on the left.

These are tank traps, *very different to the ones in Fairbourne, being much more substantial. The ones in Fairbourne are called 'Dragon's Teeth'. They were erected as part of an anti-invasion deterrent. It was thought at one time during the war that an attack was possible from the Irish Sea and that these tank traps would slow the enemy down. The view from the tiny headland at the far end of these 'traps' is spectacular, especially of Barmouth Bridge downstream.*

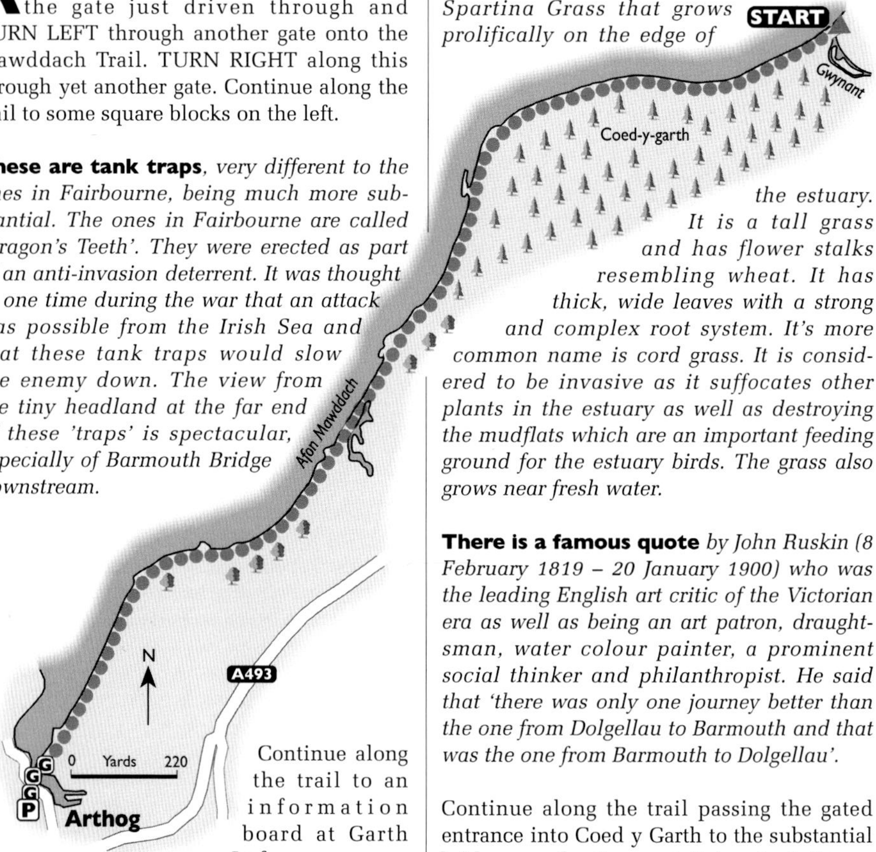

Continue along the trail to an information board at Garth Isaf.

This board *highlights the problem with Spartina Grass that grows prolifically on the edge of the estuary. It is a tall grass and has flower stalks resembling wheat. It has thick, wide leaves with a strong and complex root system. It's more common name is cord grass. It is considered to be invasive as it suffocates other plants in the estuary as well as destroying the mudflats which are an important feeding ground for the estuary birds. The grass also grows near fresh water.*

There is a famous quote *by John Ruskin (8 February 1819 – 20 January 1900) who was the leading English art critic of the Victorian era as well as being an art patron, draughtsman, water colour painter, a prominent social thinker and philanthropist. He said that 'there was only one journey better than the one from Dolgellau to Barmouth and that was the one from Barmouth to Dolgellau'.*

Continue along the trail passing the gated entrance into Coed y Garth to the substantial bridge over the Gwynant. Return to Arthog.

WALK 20

ALONG AN OLD ROAD,

CAPEL CURIG TO GLAN DENA

DESCRIPTION This is a great 8 mile journey that can be shortened as needed. There are wonderful mountain views throughout. It is not, however, recommended in very wet weather. *It is ONLY suitable for Specialist All Terrain wheelchairs as there are several rough sections.*

START The Snowdonia National Park car park at Capel Curig.

DIRECTIONS Turn off the A5 in Capel Curig either right, if coming from Bethesda, or left when coming from Betws y Coed. Go up the narrow road on the left hand side of the Pinnacle Outdoor and grocery shop past Joe Brown's climbing shop to the car park on the right just beyond the bridge over the Afon Llugwy. There are disabled toilets on the right before crossing the bridge. A RADAR key is needed for access, otherwise it is 20p.

1 Leave the car park and TURN RIGHT up the tarmac road to where it bends to the left. Continue straight ahead through the gate. A level track continues to where it rises up a short rougher section to another level section of track before going up another quite rough section. The track now descends to a more or less level track. *Over to the right is the fine pyramidal form of Pen Llithrig y Wrach 2,621 feet (799 metres).* Continue along this, with the Afon Llugwy close by to the right. Up to the left is the dark and glowering craggy form of Gallt yr Ogof, a favoured haunt of birds and occasional rock climbers. Pass through a gate just before a short line of conifers and follow a rougher section of track to reach some fir trees on the left. Pass through the gate onto a gravel track and go LEFT along it to reach a tarmac track. *Up to the left is Gwern Gof Isaf Farm, a favoured camping site for climbers and often affectionately known as 'Big Willies'. Beyond the magnificent form of Tryfan 3,002 feet (915 metres) appears in all its glory, a paradise for rock climbers. To the left of Tryfan is Glyder Fach 3,261 feet (994 metres). The twin blocks on the summit of Tryfan are easily seen and are known as 'Adam and Eve' and would you 'Adam and Eve it' that it is possible to jump from one to the other. However, in the event of a misjudgement ...*

2 Cross straight over and pass through the gate to follow the often damp track. *There is a glimpse of Carnedd Llewelyn 3,491 feet (1,064 metres) the highest peak in the Carneddau high up to the right.* Continue through a fenced section passing through a small coppice. Pass through another gate and along the grassy track that becomes gravel. Go through another gate and go up slightly and along the grassy track to reach a foot-bridge. Cross this, or for more fun, cross the ford if water levels are low! *Straight ahead is the fine form of Foel Goch 2,726 feet (831 metres).* Go through the gate and continue to go through another gate. Descend past Gwern Gof Uchaf farm, another popular campsite, to go through another gate. Follow the level track, with great views of Tryfan up to the left and the fine slab known as Tryfan Bach, through three more gates to reach the road. *Up to the right the huge bulk of Pen yr Ole Wen 3,209 feet (978 metres) looms whilst to the right of this is Carnedd Dafydd 3,425 feet (1,044 metres). The tumbling stream on the right of Pen yr Ole Wen is the Afon Lloer emanating from Cwm Lloer, a pretty cwm under the summit of Pen yr Ole Wen.*

All that remains now is the return journey.

WALK 21

THE CROSSING OF BARMOUTH BRIDGE

DESCRIPTION This is a wonderful 1¾ mile journey one way, suitable for manual wheelchairs across the amazing Pont Abermaw (Barmouth Bridge). Superb views are seen throughout both up towards the Rhinogau and the Cadair Idris range as well as a stunning vista up and down the estuary.

START At the Snowdonia National Park car park close to Morfa Mawddach rail station near the Mawddach Trail.

DIRECTIONS From Dolgellau follow the A493 towards Tywyn. Pass through the tiny hamlet of Arthog and look out for the signed right turn leading down to Morfa Mawddach rail station. Turn right down this road to the car park. There are toilets here. From the Tywyn direction, drive along the A493 and pass through Fairbourne and the left turn to the train station, shops and miniature railway. Turn left 1 mile further down to the signed Morfa Mawddach station and the car park immediately before it.

Follow the tarmac trail in front of the toilets – NOT towards the station. The track soon runs alongside the railway to where the tarmac ends at a gate. Go through onto the wooden deck, Admiring the amazing views continue to the defunct toll booth at the end of the bridge.

Either continue into Barmouth or return to Morfa Mawddach.

If continuing into Barmouth go past the toll booth at the end of the bridge to another section of tarmac path. *The toll collection became defunct in 2013.* Walk up the path to exit on to the A496. With help it is possible to go into Barmouth by TURNING LEFT along the road. The A496 is a very busy road in summer so take care following this into the town. Continue to the 'Last Inn'. TURN LEFT and follow the road along the sea front. Just beyond the Harbour Master's office TURN RIGHT up to visit the circular building known as Ty Crwn.

Ty Crwn *was erected in 1834 and was used as a jail for petty offenders and drunks. It had two sections: one for the men and the other for women. It was built on the instructions of the county's magistrates.*

Return to the sea front and TURN RIGHT. Continue to the right turn leading up to the train station from where it is possible, if desired, to catch the train back to Morfa Mawddach. It is IMPORTANT to inform the guard that you want to alight there because the station is a request stop! Or, return to Morfa Mawddach having explored the town by reversing the outward journey.

Pont Abermaw *is one of the longest timber viaducts still standing in the UK today. It is a Grade II listed structure some 699 metres long, consisting of 113 timber trestles supported by a series of cast iron pillars. It was designed by Benjamin Piercy and Henry Conybeare in 1864. Taking three years to build it was opened on the 10th October 1867. Conybeare shipped the timber in as it was much cheaper to do so than using iron. When it was first built there was a lifting drawbridge at the northern end to allow the tall ships of the day to pass up the river. However, since the railway opened there was little call for it so in 1899 it was altered to a swing bridge. Although still theoretically operational it has not been opened since 1987, when it was last tested!*

Little is known *of the history of Barmouth, or in Welsh 'Abermaw'. It is sometimes colloquially referred to as Bermo – often seen on the local buses. The dominating hill to the north of the town known as Dinas Oleu, 'The Fortress of Light'. It was settled by the Romans. Many of the scattered farmhouses date back to the 15thC whilst the older buildings in the old part of town date back to the 17thC. Barmouth developed around the shipbuilding industry until 1865, although very little if any evidence of this remains. Once trains arrived in 1867 the shipbuild-*

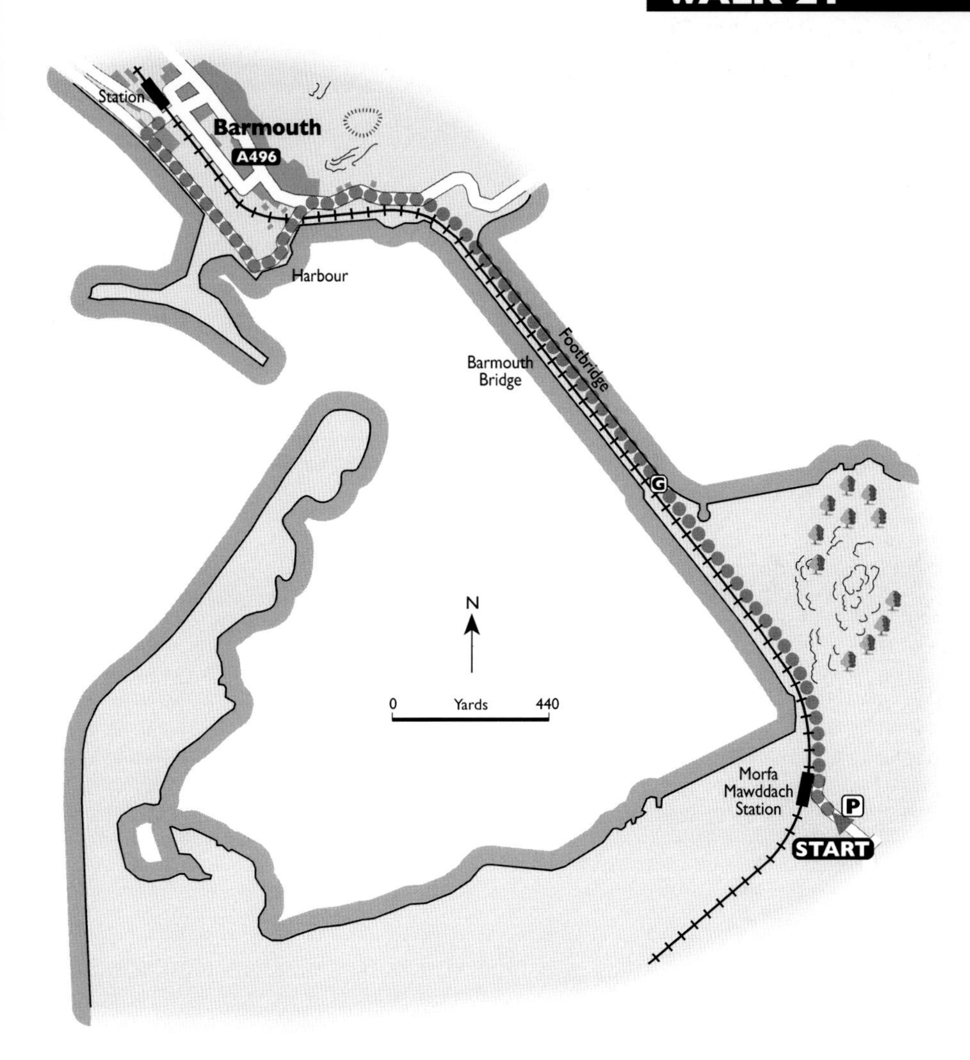

ing industry declined very quickly. In recent years Barmouth became a seaside resort, being dubbed the 'Queen of the Cambrian Coast'.

Visitors *to the area have included Charles Darwin, Percy Bysshe Shelley, and George Byron. William Wordsworth visited Barmouth in the 19thC saying: 'With a fine sea view in front, the mountains behind, the glorious estuary running eight miles inland and Cadair Idris 893 metres (2,930 feet) within compass of a day's walk, Barmouth can always hold its own against any rival'. These words wereno doubt inspired by the works of Thomas Pennant 1726 – 1798. He was a world renowned naturalist and antiquary who encouraged people to visit Wales.*

Once known as the Maw, the Mawddach Estuary was first mentioned in the 12thC by the traveller Geraldus Cambrensis. He was a cleric who went around trying to enlist people for the Crusades.

WALK 22

ARTHOG NATURE RESERVE

DESCRIPTION This is a short but pleasant I mile excursion into the RSPB reserve, an SSSI. There is much to see especially in spring and summer when butterflies are abundant. In the 1800's peat was cut here and transported over to Barmouth to keep the home fires burning. Sedge Warblers and Whitethroats are often seen and if you are lucky it is possible to see Lesser Spotted Woodpeckers and Water Rails amongst others. The trail is suitable for manual wheelchairs with help for the short descent and gate.

START At the Snowdonia National Park car park by Morfa Mawddach rail station close to the Mawddach Trail.

DIRECTIONS From Dolgellau follow the A493 towards Tywyn. Pass through the tiny hamlet of Arthog and look out for the signed right turn leading down to Morfa Mawddach rail station. Turn right down this road to the car park. There are toilets here. From the Tywyn direction, drive along the A493 and pass through Fairbourne. Turn left I mile further on down the road signed to Morfa Mawddach station and the car park immediately before it. The trail can also be accessed by train. If this method of approach is used ensure that you inform the conductor that you wish to alight at the station because it is a request stop.

From the car park follow the Mawddach Trail away from the station going past the toilets. There is a disabled one here too. Follow the tarmac track to the left of the road to reach a junction and a Snowdonia National Park plaque for the Mawddach trail.

BEAR LEFT through the gate, NOT down the dead end road, following the wide track which was once the bed of the railway line from Barmouth to Ruabon. At the junction with a path going down to the right TURN RIGHT down it and pass an information board. Although very short it is quite steep but manageable with help.

Cross a footbridge and pass through a gate. A compacted gravel path continues through woodland to a 'T' junction. TURN RIGHT and continue to another gate. Go through this to reach a tarmac road. TURN RIGHT along this to pass in front of Rhesdai St. Mary's Terrace back to the car park.

At one time *Morfa Mawddach station could lay claim to beingone of the largest stations in Wales, having five platforms. It was only superseded by Swansea and Cardiff and went under the name of Barmouth Junction at that time. In front of the toilets are the remains of a platform. The final link of the line between Dolgellau and Barmouth Junction (renamed Morfa Mawddach in 1960) opened 10 October 1867. Sadly the whole line from Barmouth to Ruabon was closed by Dr Beeching wielding his axe. On the 31st December 1964 goods traffic ceased with passenger services ceasing on the 18th January 1965. The closure eventually ensured that a wonderful scenic 8 miles-long journey could be made on foot, bicycle, horse, wheelchair and baby stroller from Morfa Mawddach to Dollgellau or in the opposite direction. It is perhaps one of the most scenic railway walks in Britain, if not the most spectacular!*

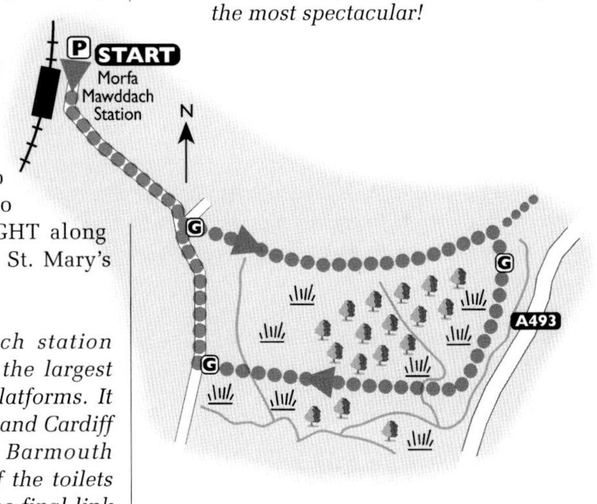

WALK 23

A ROAD RAMBLE ABOVE DOLGELLAU

DESCRIPTION Suitable for manual wheelchair users and their helpers, or preferably scooters, this is a 3½ mile circular road ramble. Fortunately the road only services the farms and is extremely quiet. Only the last 350 yards can be described as a used road as it leads to the popular car park at Ty Nant for the ascent of Cadair Idris. Scenery is varied as it goes through some pretty woodlands as well as some good views. There are some fairly steep rises which could make the journey tiresome for those pushing. Any length can be undertaken and a return made back to the start.

START At a quiet road junction along the road towards the Cadair Idris car park.

DIRECTIONS From the centre of Dolgellau follow the minor road out of town heading towards Tywyn to where a road leads up to the left, signed to Cadair Idris, can be followed for ½ mile to a wide junction with a narrow road going off to the right. There is room to park a couple of cars being mindful to park carefully and sensibly.

Go down to the left and by pass the cattle grid through the gate on the left. Continue through pretty woodland passing the right turning to Bryn y Gwin farm. The road now goes quite steeply up then much more gently to go through a gate to the left of a cattle grid. Continue to another cattle grid going through the gate on the left of it.

A level section follows before descending into a dip by Llwyniarth and rising again quite steeply to where, at the top are some extensive views.

Continue to go through a gate across the road and another by Maes Angharad Farm. A level stretch carries on and reaches another gate across the road. Pass through this and continue through a sessile oak wood and around a 90 degree bend in the road. Easier going leads past Tal y Waen Farm to reach some strange metal structures down to the left of the road. *You may well be completely flummoxed by these. They are in fact old War Department rifle range target holders!*

Go through the gate to the right of the cattle grid which is, unfortunately quite muddy in wet weather. Continue steeply up to reach another building. This one, on the left, is Gellilwyd Fawr. *This former farmhouse has a wagon entrance. The roof has graded roofing slates whilst the chimneys are typical of the Dolgellau area that have projecting slate slabs in an attempt to deflect water away from the base of the stack.*

The road now starts to descend and joins up with the Cadair Idris road. TURN LEFT and follow this road for 350 yards back to where your car is parked.

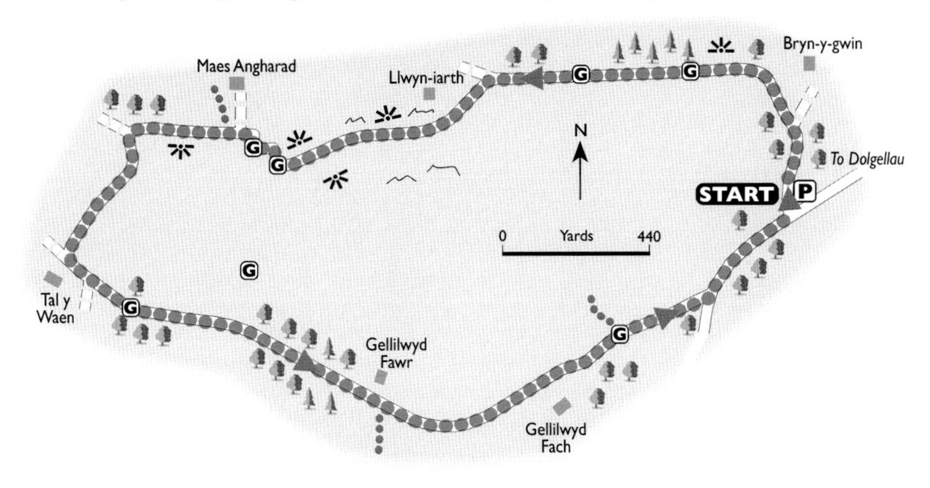

WALK 24

LLYNNAU CREGENNAN & THE FFORDD DDU

DESCRIPTION This is very scenic 6½ mile journey into a quite remote, but low, mountain area. Views are superb, especially the ones across the Mawddach Estuary. The Cregennan Lakes are extremely pretty and well worth seeing in their own right. Alternatives exist and are described in the route guide. There are some quite rough and challenging sections making it suitable ONLY for Specialist All Terrain wheelchairs..

START At the Snowdonia National Park car park for the Cregennan Lakes.

DIRECTIONS Turn off the A470 onto the A493 and drive towards Tywyn. Continue through Penmaenpool to Arthog. Turn left 250 yards beyond the sign indicating the village up the road signed to the Cregennan Lakes. This road is steep and twisty and passes through at least two gates, some may have been left open purposefully, to the car park on the right opposite the larger of the two lakes. If coming on the minor road from Dolgellau continue past the Ty Nant car park for Cadair Idris to reach a 'T' junction where a sign indicates the right turn to the Cregennan Lakes. Follow this road through two gates to reach the car park on the left.

The land around these lakes was gifted to the National Trust by Major C L Wynne-Jones in 1959 to commemorate his two sons killed in World War II. In mediaeval times there was small township here. There are also many standing stones, hut circles and cairns in the area all dating back to ancient times.

1 Go out of the car park and TURN RIGHT along the road, following the edge of the larger lake, to where it swings right and up to go through a gate. On the left some 150 yards further on a prominent standing stone can be seen. Continue through the gate and descend to a 'T' junction. TURN RIGHT. This short section of tarmac is the start of the Ffordd Ddu. Continue through another gate. Just beyond this is a farm access track going off to the right. Continue straight on to the 'Y' junction seen some 150 yards ahead.

2 TURN LEFT up the left arm of the 'Y' and follow the track. This becomes quite rough and continues up to a gate. *Note the fine standing stone silhouetted on the skyline up to the right. There is also a wonderful view of the Rhinogau forming the skyline beyond the standing stone.* Continue up the track to a gap in the wall on the right. (If desired a grassy track to the right can be followed to the standing stone by going through the gap in the wall). Keep following the rising track to go through another gate. NOTE there is a challenging gravel step just before this made by flowing water. Beyond the gate the track becomes steeper and somewhat rougher, with ruts worn by the water. Follow it up where it bends 90 degrees to the left at a track junction and continue up to a gate where the track levels.

3 Pass through the gate and continue much more easily to where the track rises and great views to the right down to the Mawddach Estuary and Barmouth. Close to the top of the rise and 100 yards beyond a finger post and down to the right a plaque can be seen set into the wall. *This commemorates the 20 airmen killed when their plane, a B-17g Flying Fortress, crashed on the 8th June 1945 on the craggy slopes of Craig Cwm-llwyd above the track to the left. They were all from the 351st Bombardment group of the USAAF on the first leg of their flight back to the USA from RAF Polebrook in Northamptonshire to RAF Valley on Anglesey.* Return from here to the 90 degree bend. At one time it was possible to take s short cut from here by going through the gate on the left and descending to the road. However, this track has become deeply rutted and it is NOT advisable to take this. Instead return to the

Craig Cwm-ll

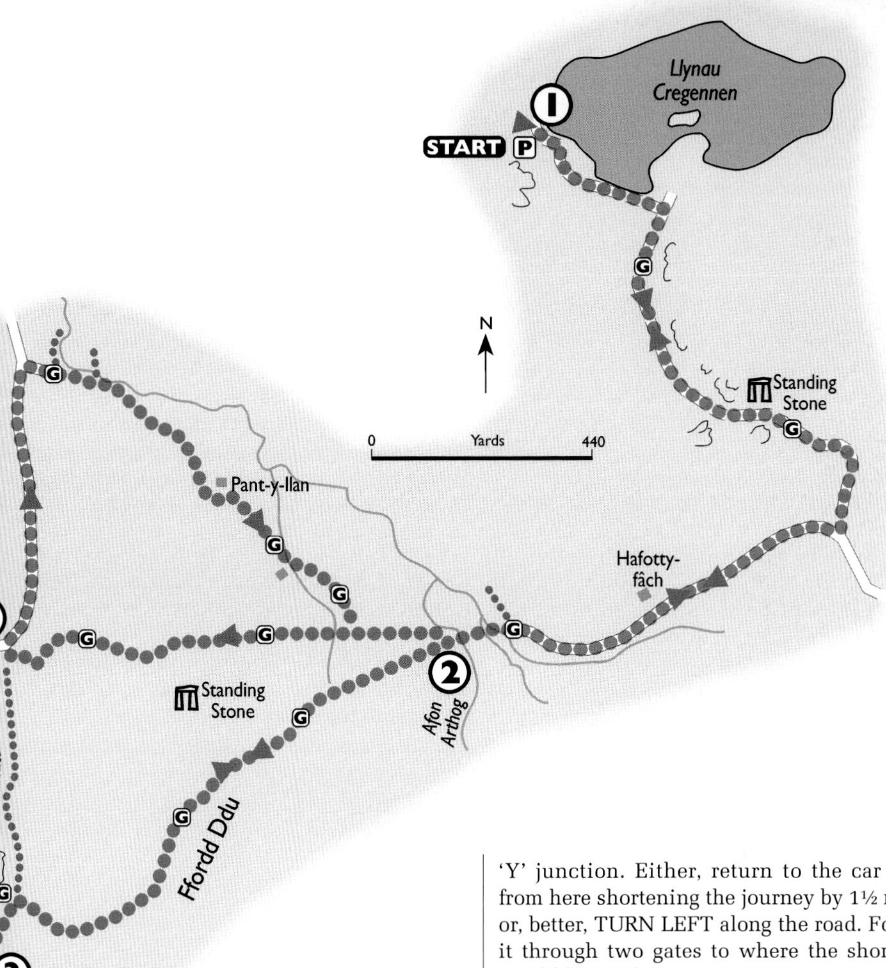

'Y' junction. Either, return to the car park from here shortening the journey by 1½ miles or, better, TURN LEFT along the road. Follow it through two gates to where the short cut would have taken you.

4 TURN RIGHT down the quite steep road. Just before the 3T weight restriction signs TURN RIGHT along the grassy track and through an old white-painted metal gate. Continue down to the Afon Arthog and a very fine clapper bridge. Continue with the river to the left to where the track bends right and up to Pant y Llan. Continue on the track above this as it starts to rise gently. When the track levels go through a gate and continue with a small larch plantation on the left. Easy going reaches another gate. Go through this and continue to the road. TURN LEFT along this back to the car park.

WALK 25

LLYN CYNWCH

DESCRIPTION This almost level 2½ miles trail walk around the lake is very pretty, especially when autumn colours are present. There is a great view of Cadair Idris. The trail can be undertaken by manual wheelchairs but there are a couple of short rough sections. Certainly not one for a solo outing! For scooter users there are a couple of sections that are uneven and care is needed to avoid tipping over, but these are passable with care.

START At the Snowdonia National Park car park for the 'Precipice Walk'.

DIRECTIONS From Dolgellau head north from town and drive over the bridge spanning the Afon Wnion and turn right. Turn left along a minor road ½ mile further, signed to Llanfachreth and the Precipice Walk. The car park is 2 miles along this road on your left. Although there are no disabled parking bays parking is free and there is an accessible toilet. It is best to park as close to the top of the car park for easier access to the exit track.

NOTE: *Due to the undersized kissing gate at the far end of Llyn Cynwch the maximum length of a wheelchair must not exceed 52 inches (132 cms). Completing just this part of the walk along the western side of the lake is still very worthwhile.*

From the top of the car park walk to the right on a level track above the car park through the wood to join a track. Follow this track first LEFT then RIGHT and down. Continue to a cottage. TURN LEFT in front of it and follow the path up and round to a kissing gate. Go through this to where the lake is seen ahead. Continue to where the path splits.

There are great views straight ahead of Cadair Idris 2,930 feet (893 metres) and Cyfrwy 2,661 feet (811 metres) to the right of it at this point. Other mountains seen from here are Rhobell Fawr 2,408 feet (734 metres) standing high above the village of Llanfachreth behind you. To the right of Rhobell Fawr in the far distance the Arans are seen. The high point of these is Aran Fawddwy 2,969 feet (905 metres).Closer to and up to the left is Foel Offrwm 1,329 feet (495 metres). At the top of this hill there is an Iron Age hill fort and a remarkable stone structure.

Go to the right towards the right hand side of the lake along a track that is a little uneven. Care is needed here to avoid tipping. Continue along the track close to the shore until a gate is reached. Go through this. Keep following the track along the edge of the lake to go through another gate. There is a superb view along the whole lake from here. The track curves round to the left over a low dam and reaches the end of a tarmac road. BEAR LEFT keeping close to the lake to go through a kissing gate. Follow the very pretty track along the lake edge to a gate. Go through this and continue to reach the kissing gate of the outward journey and return to the car park.

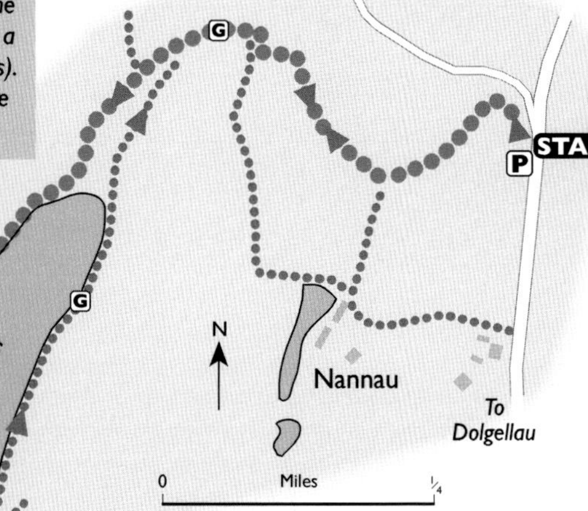

You may have noticed high and elaborate looking chimneys on many of the houses in the vicinity. They all belonged to the Nannau Estate and are a particular feature of it. Nannau Hall was built in 1693 and right up to the 1960s belonged to the large land owning family in the area, the Vaughan family.

WALK 26

LOWER DOLGOCH FALLS

DESCRIPTION A lovely ½ mile tarmac trail is quite popular, especially so in summer. The trail is suitable for manual wheelchairs, although a little help may be needed for the short rise to reach the actual waterfall. Lower Dolgoch Waterfall can be very dramatic when it is in spate after a period of heavy summer rainfall, never mind winter deluges! There is a poem on the first footbridge one of series on all the subsequent bridges. They are all reproduced below and were penned by children from the Primary School at Bryncrug.

START The car park for Dolgoch Falls on the B4405. There is a parking charge but for the disabled it is free.

DIRECTIONS From Tywyn take the A493 Dolgellau road as far as Bryncrug. Turn right here on to the B4405 signed Tal-y-llyn. The prominent car park close to the Dolgoch Hotel is on the right directly ahead up the access road before going around an almost 90 degree left hand bend in the road. This is just after a 90 degree right hand bend. When travelling from the north, turn off the A487at Minffordd on to the B4405, signed for Tywyn. Follow it by the side of Tal-y-llyn and drive through Abergynolwyn. Continue to where the road bends almost 90 degrees to the right where the car park and hotel are seen up to the left. Turn left up the access road to the car park.

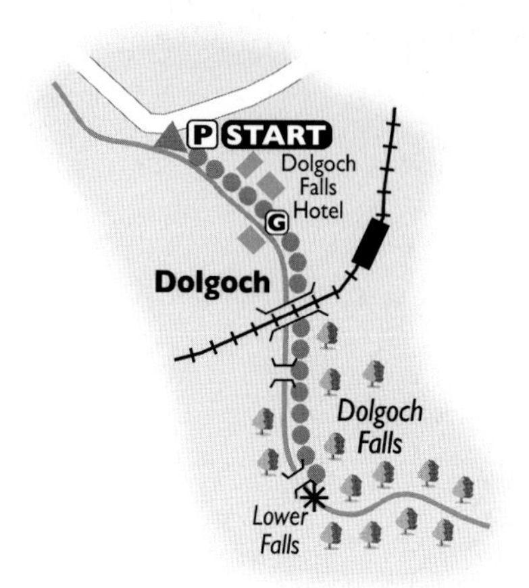

Turn left out of the car park up the narrow tarmac road passing to the right of the Dolgoch Falls Hotel. Great afternoon teas can be had here with superb cakes as well as more substantial fare. Go through the substantial metal gate ahead and keep following the tarmac track ignoring the sign to Dolgoch Station on the left. Continue up with the lively, pretty stream on the right and pass under the railway bridge carrying the Talyllyn Railway. Just beyond the bridge is a footbridge on the right, Pont Mur Mwswgl, Pont is the Welsh for bridge. Continue slightly uphill where help may be needed to the viewing area for the lower falls. There is an adit on the left here that leads into the base of a shaft. Return as for the outward journey.

The poem at Pont Mur Mwswgl reads:

'Amber iron flowing from the green moss
Damp gorge split by smooth water
The woodland welcomes
under the large arched viaduct
Follow the track ahead'

The other three bridges also have related poems.

Dolgoch Falls *were bequeathed to the public through the generosity of a Tywyn chemist, R J Roberts, at the turn of the 20thC. The viaduct passed below near the start of the walk carries the Talyllyn Railway. It was built was built at a cost of £3,000 in 1866.*

The gorge *is a veritable fern garden. The damp atmosphere from the spray of the waterfalls ensures that there are many varieties perfectly at home here including the scarce Wilson's filmy fern. There are also ten species of liverwort which in times past were believed to cure people of liver disease!*

WALK 27

TALYLLYN VIEWS

DESCRIPTION Any length of this almost level 2¾ mile tarmac road cum track can be undertaken, turning around when you have had enough. It is easily manageable by manual wheelchairs with help to open the gates. It is a scenic and pretty way to the far end of Talyllyn. The road is only used as an access for the farm along here.

START The Pen-y-Bont Hotel.

DIRECTIONS From the north or south follow the A487 to Minffordd and the junction with the B4405, signed to Tywyn. Turn onto this road. From the north this will be a right turn off the A487 and from the south it will be a left. Follow the B4405 to the lake driving alongside it to where it is possible to turn right, 350 yards beyond the Tyn y Cornel Hotel, to the Pen-y-Bont Hotel. The parking charge here is £5 which needs to be paid for in the hotel, or have a round of drinks or some food, get a receipt and display that in your car.

No description is necessary as there are no junctions, but an outline is given. Just follow the road. To start, TURN RIGHT along it. Pass the turning left into The Old Rectory B&B and follow the road through 5 gates to reach a ford. This is the furthest point that is advisable to go to, so turn around and return to Pen-y-Bont. The first section as far as Pentre Farm is the most scenic and well worth doing. It may also be all you want to do. If that is the case the distance is only 1½ miles and only two gates to open!

Talyllyn, *a glacial ribbon lake, is also known as Llyn Mwyngil or Llyn Mwyngl. The average depth is 9 feet 10 inches. It was formed by a huge post glacial landslip damming the lake in the glaciated valley. The river flowing from the lake is the Afon Dysynni and flows into the sea just to the north of Tywyn.*

Talyllyn has a stocked supply of brown trout. The fishing season for these starts in April and fishing from either a boat or on the bank is possible. Floating lines can be used due to the shallow nature of the lake. September sees the main run of sea trout and salmon. The end of the fishing season is mid-October when many sea trout and salmon are to be found in the lake, making fly fishing very interesting.

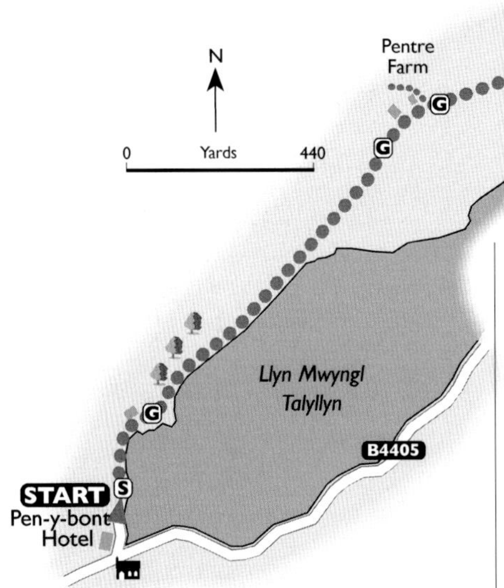

The famous *narrow gauge Talyllyn railway from Tywyn terminates not far from the end of the lake at Nant Gwernol just above the village of Abergynolwyn. A journey is definitely recommended and is easily reached by following the B4405 to Bryncrug and turning left onto the A493 into Tywyn.*

WALK 28

DOL IDRIS

DESCRIPTION This is a very pretty series of purpose made tracks totalling ¾ mile. The trail is especially colourful in autumn and there is much of interest to see as it is followed. Beautiful trees, the remains of a soft drinks laboratory, a tumbling stream and a picturesque lake with the chance to see fish jumping make this well worth exploring. There is even a tea room part way round! This trail is suitable for manual wheelchairs.

START The Snowdonia National Park car park at Minffordd.

DIRECTIONS From the north or south follow the A487 to Minffordd and the junction with the B4405, signed to Tywyn. Turn onto this road. From the north this will be a right turn off the A487 and from the south it will be a left. Immediately after turning turn right into the Snowdonia National Park car park. There are two disabled parking bays. This is a pay and display car park but free for blue badge holders. There are disabled toilets here.

Go through the gate to the right of the toilet block to a track. BEAR LEFT across this to another track. This is grassy at first and leads to a 'Y' junction. Follow the right arm of the 'Y' to reach the little lake and cross the footbridge.

Down to the left *in the outlet stream is a fish ladder. This allows salmon to reach the lake and streams further up the valley. In October when the salmon are running they can be seen jumping out of the lake in playful mood! Birds such as Dippers and Grey Wagtails breed on the lake edge.*

Follow the trail as it bends around the lake and pass by a couple of picnic tables. Just beyond is an information board explaining about the 9 species of bats found here. *Some of these found here are: Lesser Horseshoe; Daubenton's; Bechstein's and the rare Barbastelle which was recorded here in the summer of 2008, the second time ever in the Snowdonia National Park. There are approximately only 500 Barbastelles in Wales.*

TURN LEFT sharply beyond the board and follow the track through a grove of fine Spanish chestnut trees. The track rises very slightly and passes through a kissing gate. BEAR LEFT and pass in front of the café, or even have a cuppa before going further. Beyond the café is a parting of the ways having just crossed over a fine tumbling stream. *Right goes through a gate for the start of the Minffordd Path to climb Cadair Idris 2,930 feet (893 metres).* Our trail goes LEFT and down with the stream to the left. *Note the bat boxes high up on the trees down here. Just after the turning down, there are the ruins of the old 'Idris' soft drinks laboratory.*

The parkland *was donated in the 1980s by Ivor Idris whose family produced the famous ginger soft drink Idris. Nowadays the 'fiery' drink' is made by Britvic.*

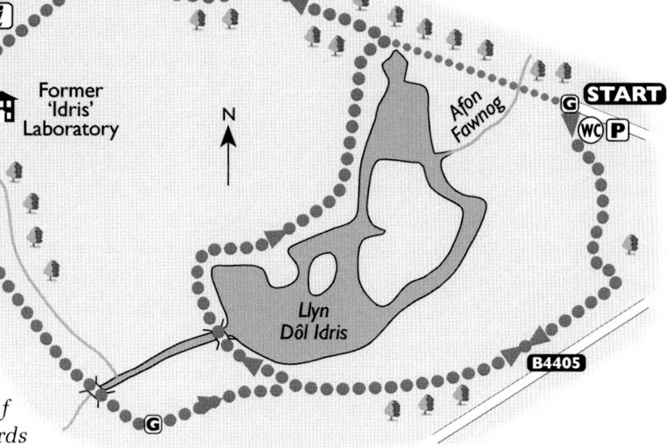

Continue down the track and cross a footbridge and continue to pass through a kissing gate. Follow the track back to the car park.

WALK 29

LLECH IDRIS CIRCULAR

DESCRIPTION This is a very scenic circular journey of 1¾ miles. The views of the Gain Valley are especially wild, giving the experience a feeling of remoteness. The Afon Gain is the river that feeds Pistyll Cain seen during the 'Waterfalls and Goldmines' trail. There is also much of historical interest. *The route is not recommended in wet weather and is only suitable for Specialist All Terrain wheelchairs. DO NOT attempt this with any other type of wheelchair.*

START At the parking space close to Pen y Stryd chapel.

DIRECTIONS Leave the A470 at Bronaber onto the minor road signed for Llanfachreth and Llanuwchllyn. Follow it up through the holiday village to the road signed for Llanuwchllyn and Abergeirw. Bear left here, the Rhiwgoch Inn is to the right, and continue up the road to a road junction. Bear right again then turn right down the dead end road to Pen y Stryd chapel and the parking area immediately before it.

The chapel *was, at one time, the main focal point for the religious well-being of the very scattered settlements in the area. It was also featured in the film about Hedd Wyn, the famous Trawsfynyyd poet.*

Hedd Wyn *was born Ellis Humphrey Evans on 13th January 1887. He died at the Battle of Passchendaele on the 31 July 1917 and posthumously awarded the Bard's Chair at the 1917 National Eistedddfod, one of several chairs he had been awarded for his poetry. He took the name Hedd Wyn, meaning blessed peace, from the way sunlight penetrated the local valleys. His themes for his poetry were inspired by nature and religion and, at the outbreak of war on the Western Front, he wrote several war poems.*

The Roman road, *Sarn Helen, goes off to the right from the chapel.*

From the parking follow the road past the chapel and graveyard. *At first this is gradually up to where there is a wonderful view of the Gain valley with the rocky form of Craig y Penamnen over to the right. On clear days the Cadair Idris ridge can be seen.* The road then goes gradually down to an obvious access track on the right with a finger post. This leads to Dol Gain. On the left of the road opposite this track is a metal gate. TURN LEFT through this onto the grassy track. *This was built over a hundred years ago by the military when they took over the whole area for military exercises.*

The well-made track continues gradually down to where Llech Idris is seen down a field to the right. It is best not to venture down the field as it is somewhat soft and wet.

This 10 feet high standing stone *is believed to date from the 2nd millennium of the Bronze Age. Little is known about it and it was not until the 17thC when it was first recorded. In legend the stone was kicked from the top of Cadair Idris, some 12 miles distant, by the giant Idris to land in a field near to Trawsfynydd. The stone lies close to an ancient road which connected the Roman forts of Tomen y Mur, north of Trawsfynydd with the one at Caer Gai near to Llyn Tegid (Lake Bala).*

Continue to go through a way marked gate and where the track descends slightly before it gradually undulates to reach a wet section. After this the track rises slightly and passes a long brick built platform to reach a road. TURN LEFT up this. Before doing so it is possible to TURN RIGHT down the road for 200 yards until just past a small on the left. Looking over to the left a low rectangular iron fence can be seen. DO NOT attempt getting to this – even though it is grassy it is very lumpy with some tussocks.

This is the grave*, dating back to the 5th or early 6thC, of Porius. On Ordnance Survey maps it is spelt Porus. The original memorial stone can be seen in the National Museum in Cardiff. It does seem strange that the grave is far removed from any church*